VINTAGE HOLLYWOOD POSTERS

Day of Sale

Saturday, December 5, 1998
4:00 pm

Feldman Gallery
PACIFIC DESIGN CENTER
8687 Melrose Avenue
West Hollywood, California 90069

Previews

November 27 – December 2
Monday – Saturday, 10:30 a.m. – 5:30 p.m.
Sunday, 12:00 noon – 5:00 p.m.
at the
HOWARD LOWERY GALLERY
3812 W. Magnolia Boulevard
Burbank, California 91505

Thursday, December 3, 4:00 pm – 8:00 pm
Friday, December 4, 11:00 am – 8:00 pm
Saturday, 10:00 am – 12:00 noon
at the
Feldman Gallery
PACIFIC DESIGN CENTER

HOWARD LOWERY
3812 W. Magnolia Blvd., Burbank, California 91505

Telephone: (818) 972–9080   Fax: (818) 972–3910

Conditions of Sale

The following conditions and other information printed in this catalogue constitute the entire terms and conditions under which Howard Lowery (hereinafter "Lowery") will offer and sell the property described herein. In conducting this auction Lowery acts solely as the agent of the seller or consignor of the property offered for sale. By placing a bid in this auction, whether in person, through an agent, by telephone, by mail, or by any other means, the buyer agrees to be bound by these conditions of sale.

1. **Conduct of the Sale.**
   a) The buyer for each lot shall be the highest bidder recognized by and acceptable to Lowery. In the event of a dispute during the auction, Lowery may, at his sole and absolute discretion, either determine the identity of the highest bidder, re-offer the lot for sale, or withdraw the lot from the sale. In the event of a dispute after the auction Lowery's sale records shall be conclusive in all respects.
   b) Lowery, as auctioneer, shall determine opening bids and bidding increments. Lowery reserves the right to withdraw any lot prior to its sale. Lowery may execute bids for absentee bidders as set forth in the following "Procedures for Bidding."
   c) All lots are sold subject to reserve prices which are the confidential minimum prices below which the lots will not be sold. Lowery or his representative may bid on each lot up to the reserve price. Consignors may not bid on their own items beyond the reserve price.
   d) Bidders are deemed to be acting as principals unless Lowery acknowledges in writing prior to the auction that the bidder is acting as an agent for another party. Unless such acknowledgment is made all bidders guarantee payment of full purchase price for all successful bids.
   e) All successful bidders agree to confirm their bids in writing upon request.
   f) Lowery reserves the right to refuse to accept bids from anyone.

2. **Responsibility for Purchased Lots.**
   Full risk and responsibility for each lot passes to the buyer at the time he or she is declared to be the highest bidder by the auctioneer. Thereafter, neither Lowery nor any of his agents or employees shall be liable for any loss or damage to the property.

3. **Purchase Price and Payment Terms.**
   a) For each lot for which the buyer is the highest bidder, the buyer shall pay the full purchase price to Lowery, which shall consist of the final bid price plus a buyer's premium, as set forth below, and any applicable sales tax.
   b) For each lot the buyer's premium shall be 15% of the final bid price. Cash, approved check or money order are accepted for payment. *Credit cards will not be accepted for payment in this auction.*
   c) All amounts and payments shall be in U.S. dollars.
   d) If payment is made by personal or business check, delivery of property purchased shall be delayed until the check has cleared the bank.
   e) Payment in full may be made during or after the auction. Subsequent to the day of the auction payment in full is due at Lowery's business address (3812 W. Magnolia Blvd., Burbank, CA 91505) within 10 calendar days of the auction. Business hours are 10:30 A.M. – 5:30 P.M., Tuesday through Saturday.
   f) For absentee bidders only, payment in full must be made within seven calendar days after receipt by the buyer of Lowery's written invoice.

4. **Remedies for Non-Payment**
   a) In the event the buyer fails to comply with the foregoing payment terms, Lowery, at his sole and absolute discretion may
         1) seek to collect payment and damages by all legal means,
         2) cancel the sale.
   b) In the event such action is necessary, Lowery may retain as liquidated damages any and all payment made by the buyer or amounts owed by Lowery to the buyer to the extent of the full purchase price.

5. **Collection of Purchased Lots**
   Property will be delivered to the buyer upon receipt by Lowery of the full purchase price at the site of the auction or at Lowery's business address (3812 W. Magnolia Blvd., Burbank, CA 91505). In the event buyer requests shipment to his or her address, Lowery or his designated agent will, at his discretion, undertake packaging and shipping services as an accommodation to the buyer. Under no circumstances will Lowery or his employees or agents be held liable for any damage to or loss of the property or for delay in delivery. The buyer agrees to pay such shipping and handling fees charged by Lowery or his agent.

6. Warranties.

a) All descriptions, illustrations, and terminology used in this catalogue represent a full effort made in good faith by Lowery to accurately represent the lots offered for sale as to origin, date, condition, and other information contained therein. Price estimates are provided solely as a guide to prospective buyers and are not intended as representations of actual values or predictions of final bid prices. All items, however, are sold "as is," and Lowery makes no express or implied warranties as to merchantability, authenticity or condition of any lot or of the correctness of the description of any lot. Prospective bidders are urged to inspect the lots personally or otherwise satisfy themselves as to the nature of each lot.

b) In the event Lowery is prevented by fire, theft or any other reason from delivering any property to the buyer, any liability of Lowery shall be limited to the amount actually paid for the property by the buyer.

c) No warranty or representation is made to the buyer that he or she acquires any copyright or reproduction rights by purchasing any lot in this auction.

7. Governing Law.

By placing a bid in the auction all buyers consent to be governed by laws of the State of California and agree that any actions arising under the terms of the auction will be determined by courts in Los Angeles County, California. This auction is conducted pursuant to California law. Howard Lowery is bonded to the State of California, office of the Secretary of State, Sacramento, California.

8. Attorney's Fees.

In the event legal action is required to enforce any of the terms contained herein the prevailing party shall be entitled to recover attorney's fees.

Procedures for Bidding

1. Bids will be accepted by mail, telephone, or in person at Lowery's business address (3812 W. Magnolia Blvd, Burbank, CA 91505) prior to the day of sale (December 5, 1998) as follows:

a) **Mail, Fax or In-Person Bids.** Written bids using Lowery's bid form must be received **no later than 6:00 p.m. on Thursday, December 3, 1998.** Bids will be executed by Lowery on behalf of the bidder up to, but not exceeding, the amount of the written bid for each lot. This service is offered as a convenience to "absentee bidders" and neither Lowery nor his agents nor employees shall be held liable for the failure to execute such bids. Identical bids for the same lot shall be executed in favor of the bid with the earliest postmark.

b) **Telephone Bids.** By prior arrangement, during the auction Lowery or his agents or employees will attempt to telephone prospective bidders who cannot attend the auction and allow them to place bids by telephone. **Prospective telephone bidders must submit to Lowery a completed and signed bid sheet (enclosed with this catalogue) listing lots in which they are interested by 6:00 p.m. on Thursday, December 3, 1998.**

The number of persons who can be telephoned to bid for a particular lot is limited. In the event more persons request to be telephoned than can be accommodated, Lowery reserves the right to contact those persons prior to the auction to determine their individual levels of interest and to decide who will be called during the auction by conducting pre-auction bidding.

Although a good faith effort will be made to reach such bidders, Lowery will not be held liable in the event that such efforts are unsuccessful. Prospective bidders are urged to make themselves available to receive telephone calls during the auction. This service is offered as a convenience to "absentee bidders" and neither Lowery nor his agents nor employees shall be held liable for the failure to execute such bids.

3. Bids will also be accepted prior to the auction in person by Lowery or his representative at Feldman Gallery of the Pacific Design Center, 8687 Melrose Avenue, West Hollywood, California 90069 during exhibition hours on Thursday, December 3.

4. Bidders who attend the auction must register with the receptionist and have in their possession a bid number issued by Lowery in order to bid. Possession of a catalogue will admit two persons to the auction. Catalogues may be purchased at the auction site.

5. This auction will be held at Feldman Gallery of the Pacific Design Center, 8687 Melrose Avenue, West Hollywood, California 90069. Registration will commence at 2:00 pm; the auction will start at 4:00 pm.

GLOSSARY

LOBBY CARD–11 x 14 in., heavy board stock. Originally made in sets of eight. Most sets have one title card which gives production credits and may be primarily artwork. The other seven cards are colored photographic scenes. Few intact sets survive.

WINDOW CARD–22 x 14 in., heavy board stock. Has blank area at top of card, where theatres would place their name and playdates.

HALF-SHEET–22 x 28 in., heavy stock. Most often with a horizontal and a vertical fold.

INSERT–36 x 14in., heavy stock. Most often found with two horizontal folds.

ONE-SHEET–41 x 27 in., (approximate), paper stock. Virtually always found with two horizontal folds and one vertical fold.

THREE-SHEET–81 x 41 in. (approximate), paper stock. Printed on two or three separate sheets, designed to overlap. As these were often posted on walls, they are much rarer than one-sheets. Very few survive from the pre-1940 period.

SIX-SHEET–81 x 81 in. (approximate), paper stock. Printed on four separate sheets, designed to overlap. As these were almost always posted on walls, they are even rarer than three-sheets. Very few survive from the pre-1940 period.

FOREIGN POSTERS– Varying sizes, depending on country of origin, paper stock.

LINEN BACKED–Poster has been mounted onto Japanese rice paper and then onto linen, in most cases.

PAPER BACKED–Poster has been mounted onto Japanese rice paper.

CONDITION GLOSSARY

Note that this grading system is significantly changed from the grading system used in Bruce Hershenson's previous auctions. It has been expanded from three grades to seven (including pluses and minuses) to give the prospective buyer a better understanding of the exact condition of what he is about to purchase. Bruce is known throughout the hobby as an extremely harsh grader! Also because over half of the lots in the auction are unrestored, there are separate guidelines for restored and unrestored posters (see below):

For unrestored posters:

Condition A: Outstanding
Posters have bright colors and are generally free from defects, but may have small tears (usually along the folds) and very tiny areas of paper loss (such as pinholes) that do not materially affect the image, and are easily restored if desired.

Condition B: Average
Posters are in average used condition. They may have minor defects, including some of the following: tears, slight paper loss, minor staining, slight fading, tape on reverse.

Condition C: Below Average
Posters have significant defects, such as paper loss that extends into the artwork, major fading, major staining, etc. Please note that there are no Condition C unrestored posters in this auction.

For restored posters:
(Note that almost all restored posters receive a maximum grade of B+; generally, a restored poster in B+ condition will be acceptable to virtually all collectors):

Condition A: Outstanding. Posters have bright colors and very minor restoration, confined to the borders and folded areas.

Condition B: Average. Posters have more restoration at folds and borders, and may have minor restoration in other areas.

Condition C: Below Average. Posters required significant overall restoration. Although the poster originally had major defects, it has now had expert restoration and has a good overall appearance.

Because posters are much more complex than many other collectibles it is difficult to fit them into a simple grading system. Prospective buyers are urged to examine the posters for themselves, especially if a lot receives a grade of B, B-, C+, or C. Generally a lot receiving a grade of B+, A-, or A will be acceptable to virtually all collectors.

Note: All of the posters in this catalog were photographed by David Graveen of Acme Movie Posters. The catalog was prepared by Bruce Hershenson, Sylvia Hershenson, and Courier Graphics, and was published by Bruce Hershenson.

The most popular cowboy star of the 1920s was Tom Mix. He made only 9 sound films, and one-sheets from them are extremely rare and desired by collectors.

1 **Destry Rides Again**, Universal, 1932, one-sheet, Cond. B+, linenbacked, 41 x 27 in $2,000-3,000

The greatest (and most collected) cowboy star of all time is John Wayne. **The Man From Monterey** has an excellent image of the very young John Wayne, prior to his many successes.

2 **The Man From Monterey**, First National, 1933, one-sheet, Cond. B+, linenbacked, 41 x 27 in
$3,000-5,000

3 **Lawless Range**, Republic, 1935, half-sheet, Cond. B+, 22 x 28 in
$800-1,000

4 **Westward Ho**, Republic, 1935, half-sheet, Cond. B, 22 x 28 in
$700-900

5 **Overland Stage Raiders**, Republic, 1938, half-sheet, Cond. B+, 22 x 28 in
$400-600

6 **The Shepherd of the Hills**, Paramount, 1941, insert, Cond. B+, 36 x 14 in
$150-250

7 **West of the Divide**, Lone Star, undated reissue, insert, Cond. A-, 36 x 14 in
$75-150

Roy Rogers' nickname was the "King of the Cowboys". His very first film was **Under Western Stars** in 1938, and poster material from this film is extremely difficult to obtain.

8 **Under Western Stars**, Republic, 1938, one-sheet, Cond. B+, linenbacked, 41 x 27 in $1,500-2,000

9 **In Old Caliente,** Republic, 1939, one-sheet, Cond. B, 41 x 27 in $1,500-2,000

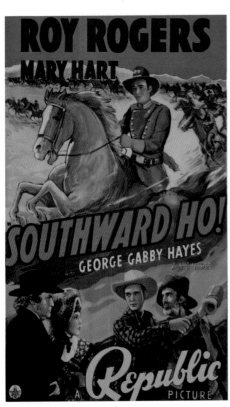

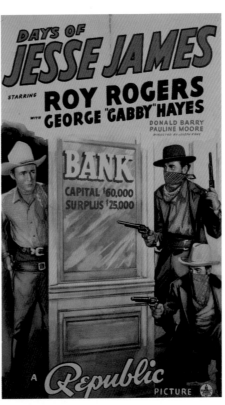

10 **Southward Ho**, Republic, 1939, one-sheet, Cond. B, 41 x 27 in $500-700

11 **Days of Jesse James**, Republic, 1939, one-sheet, Cond. B, 41 x 27 in $500-700

12 **Jesse James at Bay**, Republic, 1941, one-sheet, Cond. B+, linenbacked, 41 x 27 in $500-700

In recent years, Roy Rogers posters have become very hard to find, as most have "vanished" into private collections. Never before have so many of Roy's posters been offered at one time.

13 **The Arizona Kid,** Republic, 1939, one-sheet, Cond. B+, linenbacked, 41 x 27 in $1,500-2,000

14 **Saga of Death Valley**, Republic, 1939, one-sheet, Cond. A-, linenbacked, 41 x 27 in $1,000-1,500

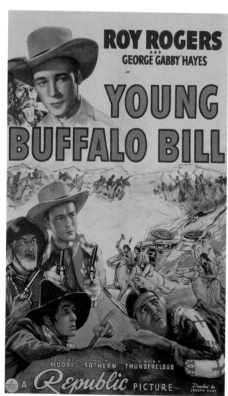

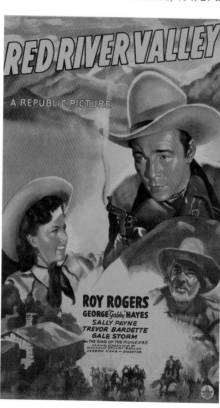

15 **Young Buffalo Bill**, Republic, 1940, one-sheet, Cond. B+, linenbacked, 41 x 27 in $500-700

16 **Red River Valley**, Republic, 1941, one-sheet, Cond. B, 41 x 27 in $500-700

17 **Nevada City**, Republic, 1941, one-sheet, Cond. B, 41 x 27 in $500-700

The Roy Rogers posters in this auction come from a single collection that was formed over many years. If kept intact it would represent one of the finest collections of Rogers' material there is.

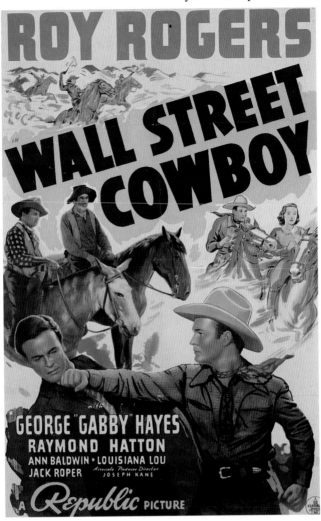

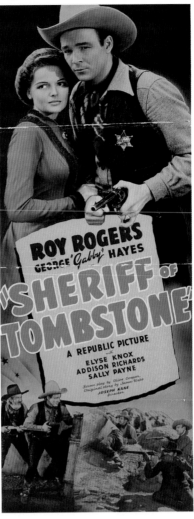

18 **Wall Street Cowboy**, Republic, 1939, one-sheet, Cond. B+, 41 x 27 in $600-800

19 **Wall Street Cowboy**, Republic, 1939, insert, Cond. A, 36 x 14 in $200-300

20 **Sheriff of Tombstone**, Republic, 1941, insert, Cond. B, 36 x 14 in $150-300

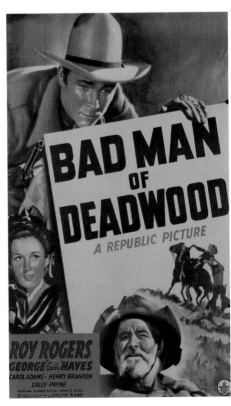

21 **Bad Man of Deadwood**, Republic, 1941, one-sheet, Cond. B+, 41 x 27 in $400-600

22 **In Old Cheyenne**, Republic, 1941, one-sheet, Cond. B, 41 x 27 in $400-600

23 **Ridin' Down the Canyon**, Republic, 1942, one-sheet, Cond. A-, 41 x 27 in $500-700

In the 1940s some filmmakers added beautiful women into western films, no matter how implausible the result. Top beauties such as Gene Tierney and Jane Russell had leading roles.

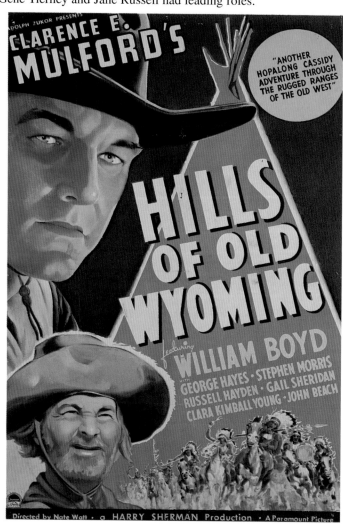

24 The Carson City Kid, Republic, 1940, half-sheet, Cond. B+, 22 x 28 in $200-400

25 High Noon, United Artists, 1952, half-sheet, Cond. B, 22 x 28 in $200-400

26 Hills of Old Wyoming, Paramount, 1937, one-sheet, Cond. B+, 41 x 27 in $500-700

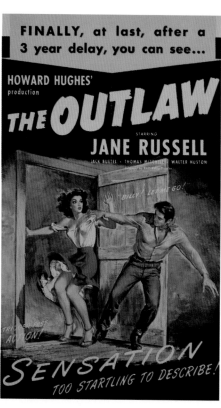

27 Belle Starr, 20th Century Fox, 1941, one-sheet, Cond. A-, 41 x 27 in $500-700

28 The Outlaw, RKO, R1950, one-sheet, Cond. B, 41 x 27 in $400-600

29 The Trail Drive, Universal, 1933, one-sheet, Cond. A, 41 x 27 in $500-700

Ken Maynard made a staggering number of films in the early 1930s. He was the epitome of the 1930s action hero, with his square jaw and ten gallon hat, always ready to battle injustice.

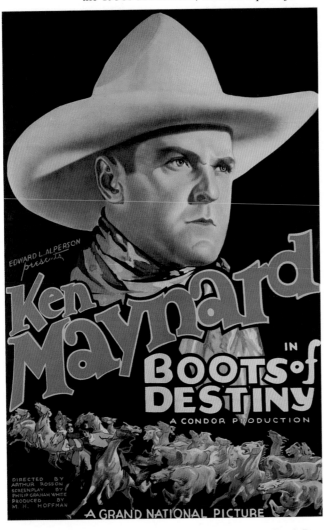

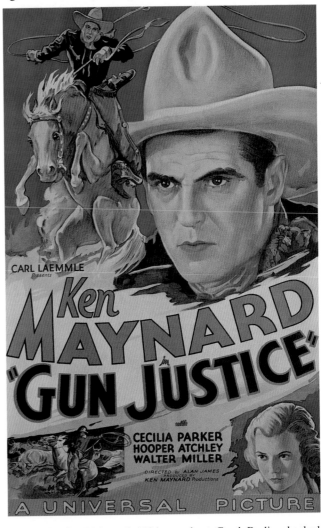

30 Boots of Destiny, Grand National, 1937, one-sheet, Cond. B+, linenbacked, 41 x 27 in $700-900

31 Gun Justice, Universal, 1934, one-sheet, Cond. B, linenbacked, 41 x 27 in $700-900

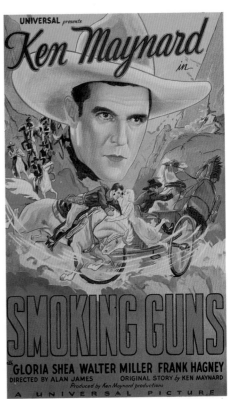

32 The Wagon Master, Universal, 1929, one-sheet, Cond. A-, 41 x 27 in $600-800

33 Fargo Express, Tiffany, 1932, one-sheet, Cond. B+, linenbacked, 41 x 27 in $500-700

34 Smoking Guns, Universal, 1934, one-sheet, Cond. B+, 41 x 27 in $700-900

A separate poster was created for each chapter of serials, and it is difficult to find more than one poster from any serial. Remarkably, all of the posters from two different serials are offered here!

35 **Mystery Mountain**, Mascot, 1934, 12 one-sheets (2 pictured) and set of 8 lobby cards (2 pictured), Cond. A to B, 41 x 27 in and 11 x 14 in $5,000-7,000

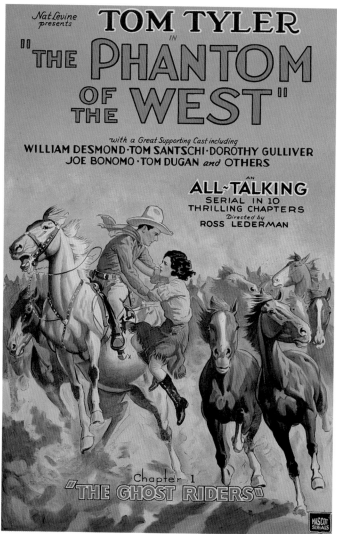

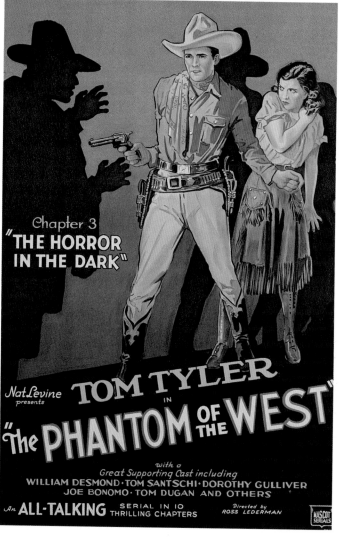

36 **The Phantom of the West,** Mascot, 1930, 10 one-sheets (2 pictured), Cond. A (8 are unfolded), each 41 x 27 in $4,000-6,000

Offered on this and following pages is an unparalleled collection of original Tim McCoy and Buck Jones posters from the 1930s. If kept intact, it would certainly be the finest single collection of these posters.

37 **Silent Men**, Columbia, 1933, one-sheet, Cond. B+, linenbacked, 41 x 27 in $900-1,200

39 **The Fighting Fool**, Columbia, 1932, three-sheet, Cond. B+, linenbacked, 81 x 41 in $1,500-2,500

38 **Two Fisted Law**, Columbia, 1932, one-sheet, Cond. B, linenbacked, 41 x 27 in $900-1,200

It is fortunate for poster collectors that Tim McCoy and Buck Jones worked for Columbia Studios in the early 1930s, which used stone lithography to create memorable posters for each of their films.

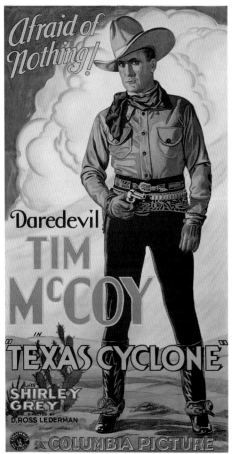

40 **Texas Cyclone**, Columbia, 1932, three-sheet, Cond. B, linenbacked, 81 x 41 in $1,000-1,500

41 **Daring Danger**, Columbia, 1932, three-sheet, Cond. B+, linenbacked, 81 x 41 in $1,000-1,500

42 **Cornered**, Columbia, 1933, three-sheet, Cond. B-, linenbacked, 81 x 41 in $1,000-1,500

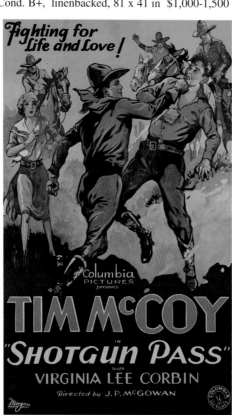

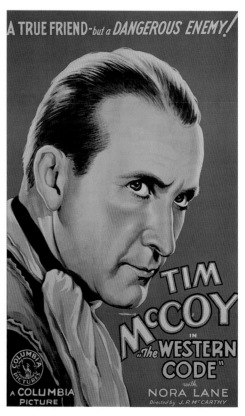

43 **Rusty Rides Alone**, Columbia, 1933, one-sheet, Cond. B+, linenbacked, 41 x 27 in $800-1,000

44 **Shotgun Pass**, Columbia, 1931, one-sheet, Cond. B+, linenbacked, 41 x 27 in $700-900

45 **The Western Code**, Columbia, 1932, one-sheet, Cond. B+, 41 x 27 in $700-900

For each B-Western film the studios would usually create only a one-sheet, three-sheet, and insert poster.
Three-sheets are extremely rare, yet this auction contains 15 Tim McCoy and Buck Jones three-sheets!

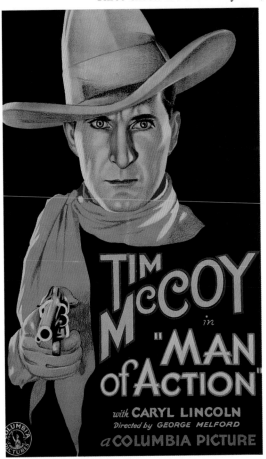

46 **Man of Action**, Columbia, 1932, one-sheet,
Cond. B, linenbacked, 41 x 27 in $1,000-1,500

47 **Man of Action**, Columbia,
1932, insert, Cond. B+,
36 x 14 in $300-500

48 **Fighting Shadows**, Columbia, 1935, one-sheet,
Cond. B+, linenbacked, 41 x 27 in $500-700

49 **Man of Action**, Columbia, 1932,
three-sheet, Cond. B+, linenbacked,
81 x 41 in $900-1,200

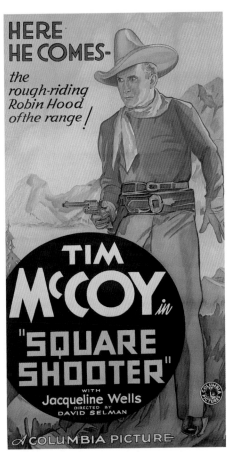

50 **Square Shooter**, Columbia, 1935,
three-sheet, Cond. B+, linenbacked,
81 x 41 in $1,000-1,500

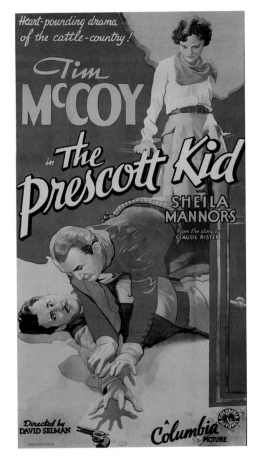

51 **The Prescott Kid**, Columbia, 1934, three-
sheet, Cond. B+, linenbacked, 81 x 41 in
                          $900-1,200

In **White Eagle** Buck Jones played a native American, something rarely done by the cowboy stars of the 1930s. This casting resulted in very striking images for both posters from this film.

52 **White Eagle**, Columbia, 1932, one-sheet, Cond. B+, linenbacked, 41 x 27 in $1,500-2,000

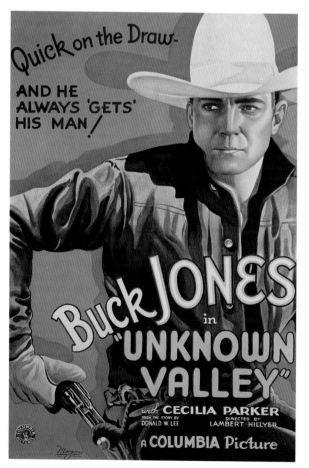

53 **Unknown Valley**, Columbia, 1933, one-sheet, Cond. B, linenbacked, 41 x 27 in $1,000-1,500

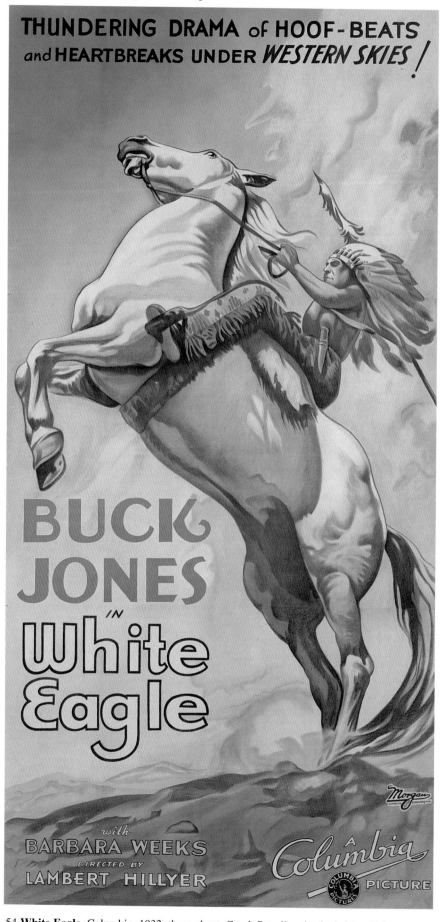

54 **White Eagle**, Columbia, 1932, three-sheet, Cond. B+, linenbacked, 81 x 41 in
$1,500-2,500

The one-sheet for **South of the Rio Grande** is considered one of the finest of all B-Western movie posters. The three-sheet from the same film has never before been offered for sale.

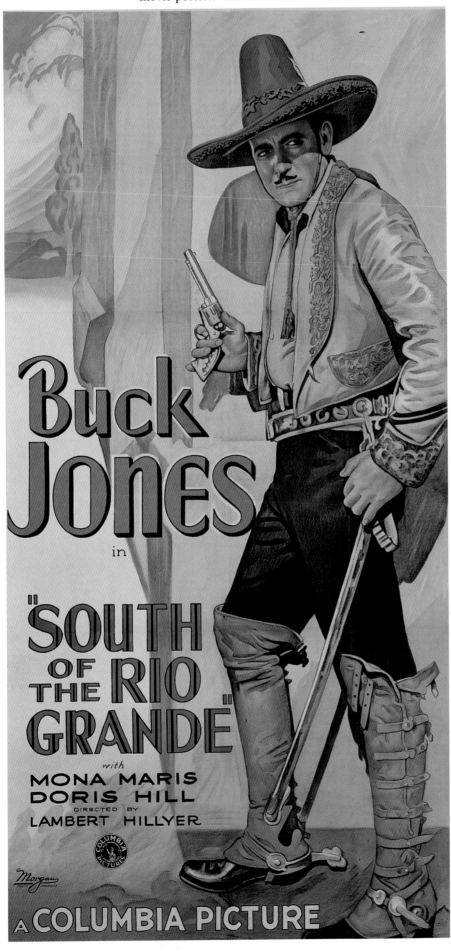

56 **South of the Rio Grande,** Columbia, 1932, one-sheet, Cond. B+, linenbacked, 41 x 27 in $2,000-3,000

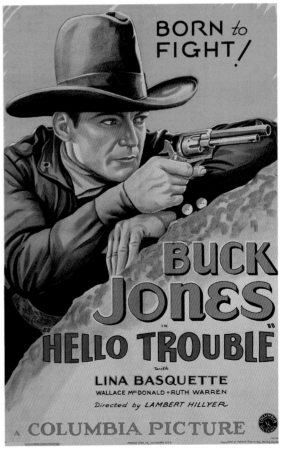

55 **South of the Rio Grande,** Columbia, 1932, three-sheet, Cond. B, linenbacked, 81 x 41 in $1,500-2,500

57 **Hello Trouble**, Columbia, 1932, one-sheet, Cond. B, linenbacked, 41 x 27 in $1,000-1,500

It is rare that more than two 1930s Buck Jones posters are offered in a single auction.
Remarkably, this auction contains 26 Buck Jones posters from the 1930s!!

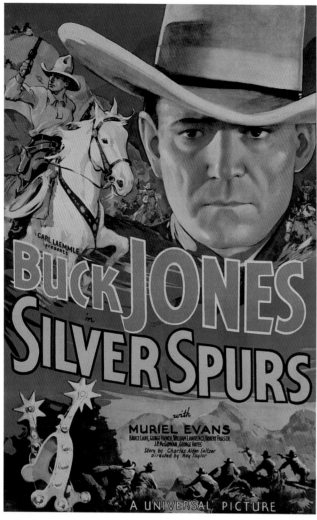

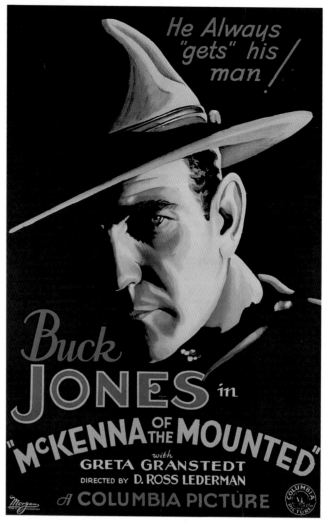

58 **Silver Spurs**, Universal, 1936, one-sheet, Cond. B, linenbacked, 41 x 27 in $900-1,200

59 **McKenna of the Mounted**, Columbia, 1932, one-sheet, Cond. B+, 41 x 27 in $900-1,200

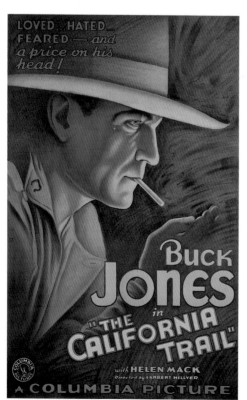

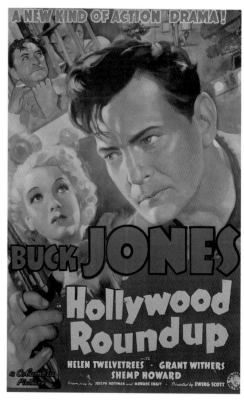

60 **The California Trail**, Columbia, 1933, one-sheet, Cond. B+, linenbacked, 41 x 27 in $900-1,200

61 **Treason**, Columbia, 1933, one-sheet, Cond. B+, linenbacked, 41 x 27 in $900-1,200

62 **Hollywood Roundup**, Columbia, 1937, one-sheet, Cond. B+, 41 x 27 in $800-1,000

For B-Westerns, Columbia usually made only one-sheet, three-sheet and insert posters. It is extremely rare for all the different posters to be offered at one time, as are those of **One Man Law**.

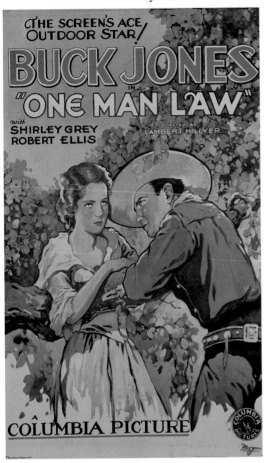

63 **One Man Law**, Columbia, 1932, one-sheet, Cond. B+, 41 x 27 in $900-1,200

64 **One Man Law**, Columbia, 1932, insert, Cond. C+, 36 x 14 in $100-200

65 **The Fighting Code**, Columbia, 1933, one-sheet, Cond. B-, 41 x 27 in $600-800

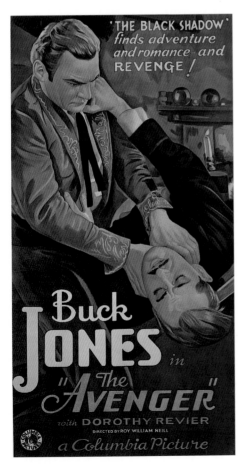

66 **The Avenger**, Columbia, 1931, three-sheet, Cond. B, linenbacked, 81 x 41 in $900-1,200

67 **One Man Law**, Columbia, 1932, three-sheet, Cond. B+, linenbacked, 81 x 41 in $900-1,200

68 **The Fighting Code**, Columbia, 1933, three-sheet, Cond. B, linenbacked, 81 x 41 in $900-1,200

After being Columbia Studios' top western star for several years, Buck Jones signed
with arch rival Universal Studios, and made a long series of similar films for them.

69 **Outlawed Guns**, Universal, 1935, one-sheet, Cond. B+,
linenbacked, 41 x 27 in $900-1,200

70 **Boss Rider of Gun Creek**, Universal, 1936, one-sheet,
Cond. B+, linenbacked, 41 x 27 in $900-1,200

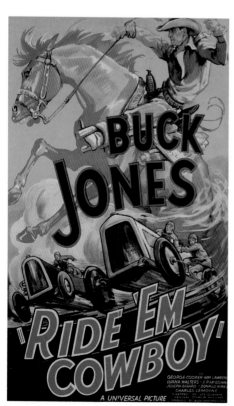

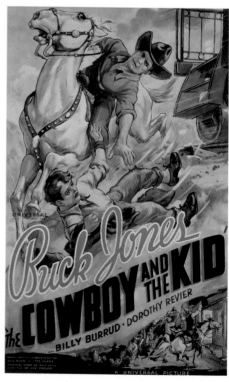

71 **Ride 'Em Cowboy**, Universal, 1936,
one-sheet, Cond. B+, 41 x 27 in $900-1,200

72 **For the Service,** Universal, 1936, one-sheet,
Cond. A, 41 x 27 in $900-1,200

73 **The Cowboy and the Kid**, Universal,
1936, one-sheet, Cond. B+, linenbacked,
41 x 27 in $900-1,200

Whereas Buck Jones' Columbia posters were often close-ups of the star, Universal's posters usually had several images, showing multiple scenes from the film.

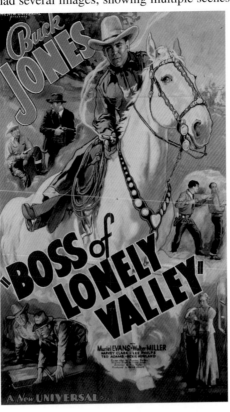

74 **The Man Trailer,** Columbia, 1934, one-sheet, Cond. B, linenbacked, 41 x 27 in $900-1,200

75 **Boss of Lonely Valley**, Universal, 1937, one-sheet, Cond. A-, 41 x 27 in $900-1,200

76 **Smoke Tree Range**, Universal, 1937, one-sheet, Cond. A-, 41 x 27 in $900-1,200

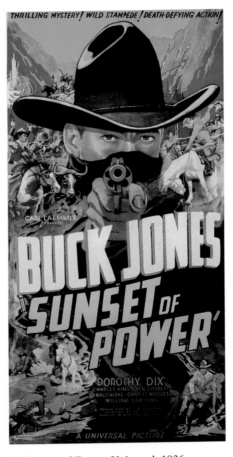

77 **The Man Trailer,** Columbia, 1934, three-sheet, Cond. B+, linenbacked, 81 x 41 in $1,000-1,500

78 **Sunset of Power,** Universal, 1936, three-sheet, Cond. B, linenbacked, 81 x 41 in $1,000-1,500

79 **Stone of Silver Creek**, Universal, 1935, three-sheet, Cond. B+, linenbacked, 81 x 41 in $1,000-1,500

In 1934, Columbia Studios reissued many of Buck Jones' westerns from the preceding years, with entirely different artwork, often equaling or surpassing the original posters.

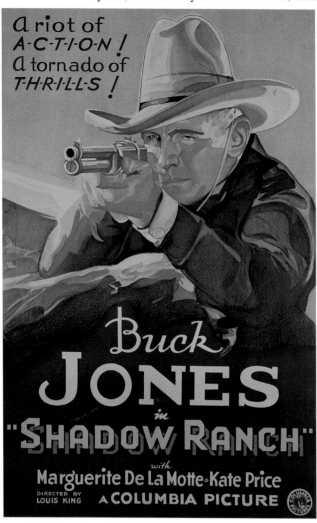

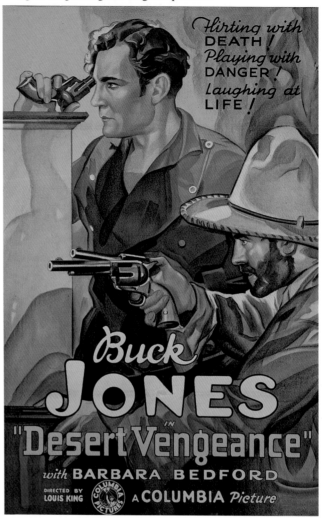

80 **Shadow Ranch**, Columbia, 1934 reissue, one-sheet, Cond. B+, linenbacked, 41 x 27 in $500-700

81 **Desert Vengeance**, Columbia, 1934 reissue, one-sheet, Cond. B, 41 x 27 in $500-700

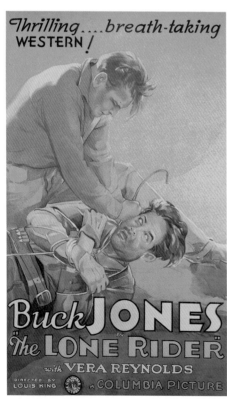

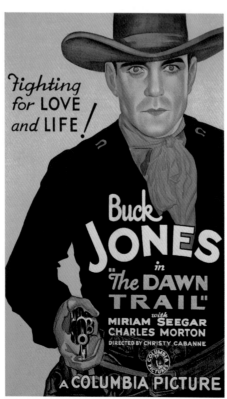

82 **The Lone Rider,** Columbia, 1934 reissue, one-sheet, Cond. B, linenbacked, 41 x 27 in $400-600

83 **The Dawn Trail**, Columbia, 1934 reissue, one-sheet, Cond. B, linenbacked, 41 x 27 in $500-700

84 **The Lone Trail**, Webb Douglas, 1932, one-sheet, Cond. A, 41 x 27 in $200-400

In the1930s westerns were so popular that just about every major star made at least one, including tough guy James Cagney, and Richard Dix, who had been so memorable in Cimarron.

85 **The Oklahoma Kid**, Warner Brothers, 1939, one-sheet, Cond. B, 41 x 27 in $1,000-1,500

86 **The Arizonian**, RKO, 1935, one-sheet, Cond. B+, linenbacked, 41 x 27 in $900-1,200

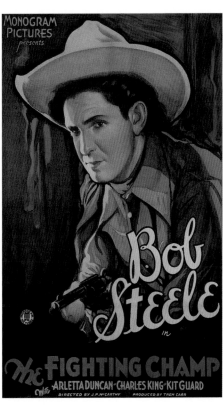

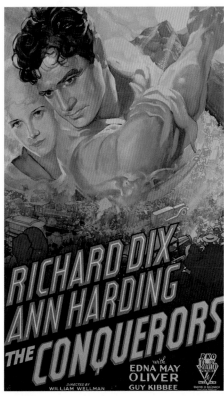

87 **Ramona**, 20th Century Fox, 1936, one-sheet, Cond. B, linenbacked, 41 x 27 in $600-800

88 **The Fighting Champ**, Monogram, 1932, one-sheet, Cond. B, linenbacked, 41 x 27 in $500-700

89 **The Conquerors**, RKO, 1932, one-sheet, Cond. B, 41 x 27 in $500-700

Gene Autry was the first of the great singing cowboys, and he maintained his immense popularity throughout the 1930s and 1940s in spite of intense competion from friendly rival Roy Rogers.

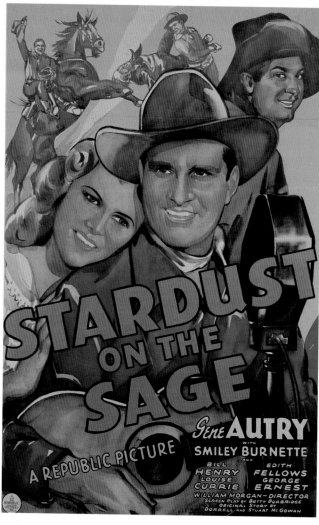

90 **Ridin' on a Rainbow**, Republic, 1941, one-sheet, Cond. B, 41 x 27 in $600-800

91 **Stardust on the Sage**, Republic, 1942, one-sheet, Cond. B, 41 x 27 in $600-800

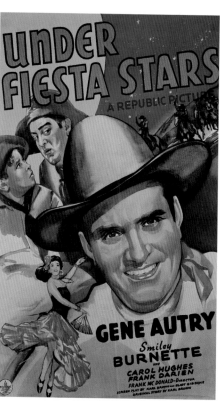

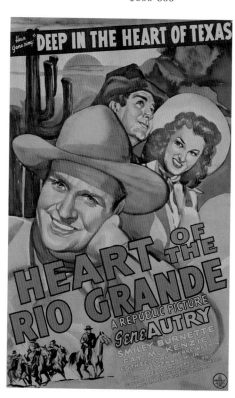

92 **The Singing Hill**, Republic, 1941, one-sheet, Cond. B+, linenbacked, 41 x 27 in $500-700

93 **Under Fiesta Stars**, Republic, 1941, one-sheet, Cond. B, 41 x 27 in $500-700

94 **Heart of the Rio Grande,** Republic, 1942, one-sheet, Cond. B, linenbacked, 41 x 27 in $500-700

Zane Grey was the early 20th century's answer to Stephen King or John Grisham, with scores of films based on his writings. Rex Bell was a great cowboy star, and also Clara Bow's husband.

95 **Tumbling Tumbleweeds**, Republic, undated reissue, one-sheet, Cond. B+, linenbacked, 41 x 27 in $400-600

96 **Diamond Trail**, Monogram, 1932, one-sheet, Cond. B+, 41 x 27 in $500-700

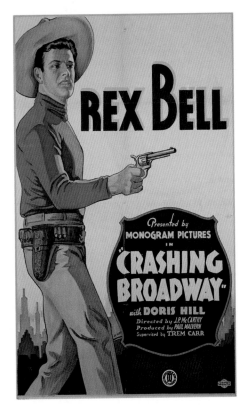

97 **Nevada**, Paramount, 1935, one-sheet, Cond. A-, 41 x 27 in $500-700

98 **Rocky Mountain Mystery**, Paramount, 1935, one-sheet, Cond. B+, 41 x 27 in $500-700

99 **Crashing Broadway**, Monogram, 1933, one-sheet, Cond. B+, 41 x 27 in $400-600

Three of the most desirable Marilyn Monroe posters are offered here. Ingrid Bergman began by making films in her native Sweden, and one of them, **Intermezzo**, was remade for her U.S debut.

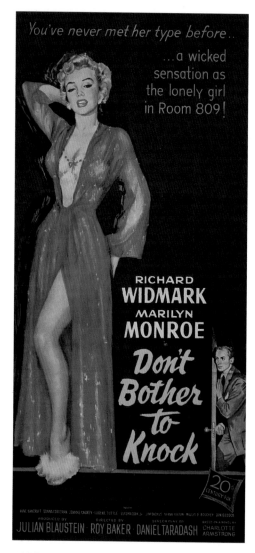

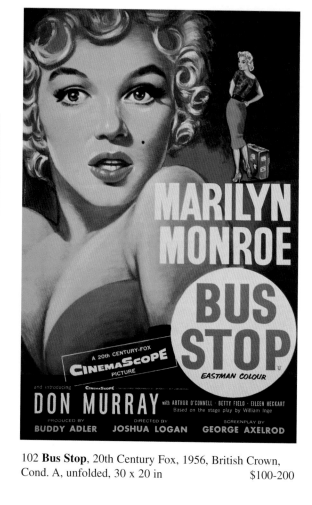

102 **Bus Stop**, 20th Century Fox, 1956, British Crown, Cond. A, unfolded, 30 x 20 in $100-200

100 **Don't Bother to Knock**, 20th Century Fox, 1952, three-sheet, Cond. B-, linenbacked, 81 x 41 in $1,000-1,500

101 **The Asphalt Jungle**, MGM, 1950, insert, Cond. B+, 36 x 14 in $300-500

104 **Joan of Arc**, RKO, 1948, one-sheet, Cond. B+, linenbacked, 41 x 27 in $400-600

103 **Intermezzo**, Svensk, 1936, Swedish poster, Cond. A, linenbacked, 47 x 102 in $1,000-1,500

The poster designer for the one-sheet for **This Gun For Hire** chose to depict Veronica Lake and fourth-billed Alan Ladd, which resulted in one of the most admired film posters ever created.

105 **This Gun for Hire**, Paramount, 1942, one-sheet, Cond. B+, linenbacked, 41 x 27 in $4,000-6,000

Perhaps it was due to the depressing realities of World War II, but the early 1940s cinema produced dozens of memorable film noirs, including several directed by the great Alfred Hitchcock.

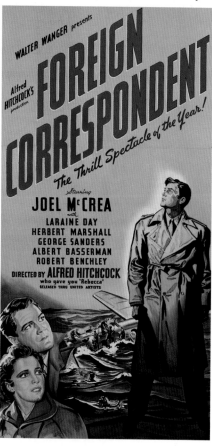

106 **This Gun for Hire**, Paramount, 1942, insert, Cond. A-, 36 x 14 in
$1,000-1,500

107 **Foreign Correspondent**, United Artists, 1940, three-sheet, Cond. A, linenbacked, 81 x 41 in
$1,000-1,500

108 **Notorious**, RKO, 1946, insert, Cond. A, 36 x 14 in
$500-700

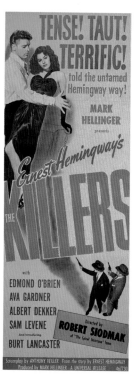

109 **Spellbound**, United Artists, 1945, insert, Cond. B+, 36 x 14 in
$400-600

110 **Gaslight**, MGM, 1944, insert, Cond. A, 36 x 14 in
$150-300

111 **The Killers**, Universal, 1946, insert, Cond. B+, 36 x 14 in
$100-200

112 **Sorry, Wrong Number**, Paramount, 1948, insert, Cond. A, 36 x 14 in
$100-200

The most popular Charlie Chan films are those which feature Warner Oland in the lead role.
Laura and **The Blue Dahlia** are well-regarded film noirs that are highly collectible poster titles.

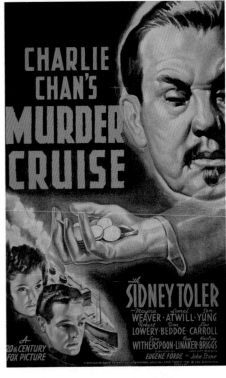

113 Charlie Chan at the Olympics,
20th Century Fox, 1937, one-sheet, Cond. B,
linenbacked, 41 x 27 in $700-900

114 Charlie Chan on Broadway,
20th Century Fox, 1937, one-sheet, Cond. B+,
linenbacked, 41 x 27 in $700-900

115 Charlie Chan's Murder Cruise,
20th Century Fox, 1940, one-sheet, Cond. B-,
41 x 27 in $500-700

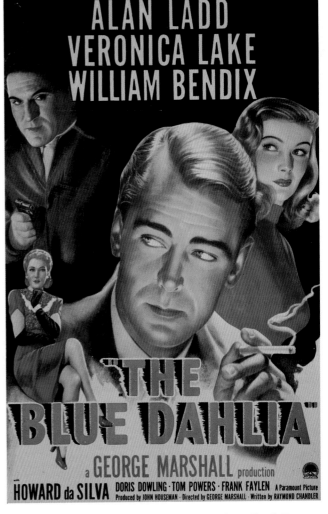

116 Laura, 20th Century Fox, 1944, one-sheet, Cond. A-,
41 x 27 in $1,500-2,500

117 The Blue Dahlia, Paramount, 1946, one-sheet, Cond. B+,
41 x 27 in $1,500-2,500

The most memorable film portrayal of Sherlock Holmes was first seen in **The Hound of the Baskervilles** in 1939, with Basil Rathbone and Nigel Bruce playing the leading roles.

118 **The Hound of the Baskervilles**, 20th Century Fox, 1939, one-sheet, Cond. A, 41 x 27 in $5,000-7,000

The first Holmes film in 1939 was so popular that a sequel was issued the same year. Over the next seven years more sequels were issued on a regular basis, always with the same leads.

119 **Sherlock Holmes and the Secret Weapon**, Universal, 1942, insert, Cond. A, unfolded, 36 x 14 in $300-500

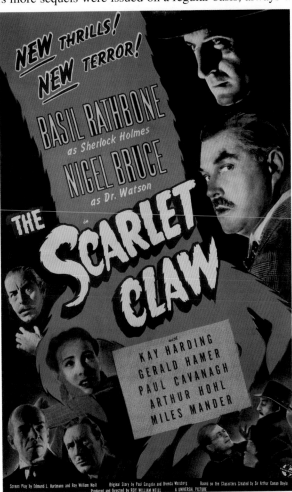

120 **The Scarlet Claw**, Universal, 1944, one-sheet, Cond. B, linenbacked, 41 x 27 in $500-700

121 **The Scarlet Claw**, Universal, 1944, insert, Cond. A-, 36 x 14 in $300-500

122 **The Pearl of Death**, Universal, 1944, one-sheet, Cond. B+, linenbacked, 41 x 27 in $600-800

123 **Terror By Night**, Universal, 1946, one-sheet, Cond. B+, linenbacked, 41 x 27 in $500-700

124 **The House of Fear**, Universal, 1944, one-sheet, Cond. B+, linenbacked, 41 x 27 in $500-700

I Love Trouble had a surprisingly risque poster at a time when posters were normally very sedate.
Peter Lorre is best-remembered as a character actor, but he had the lead in several 1930s films.

125 **The House of Fear**, Universal, 1944 , half-sheet,
Cond. B+, linenbacked, 22 x 28 in $300-500

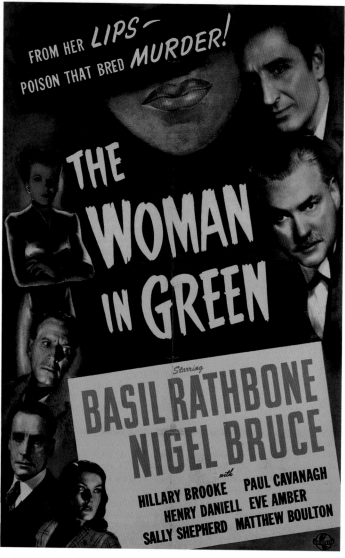

126 **The Woman in Green**, Universal, 1945, half-sheet,
Cond. B+, 22 x 28 in $200-400

127 **The Woman in Green**, Universal, 1945, one-sheet, Cond. A-,
41 x 27 in $500-700

128 **I Love Trouble**, Columbia, 1947,
one-sheet, Cond. A, 41 x 27 in $500-700

129 **Crack-Up**, 20th Century Fox, 1936,
one-sheet, Cond. B+, linenbacked,
41 x 27 in $500--700

130 **Lancer Spy**, 20th Century Fox,
1937, one-sheet, Cond. B+, linenbacked,
41 x 27 in $500-700

The popularity of Charlie Chan inspired the **Mr. Moto** series, starring Peter Lorre. **The Postman Always Rings Twice** and **Double Indemnity** were among the finest film noirs ever made.

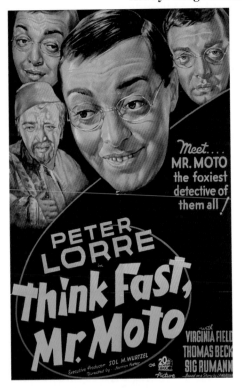

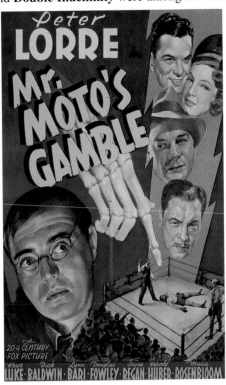

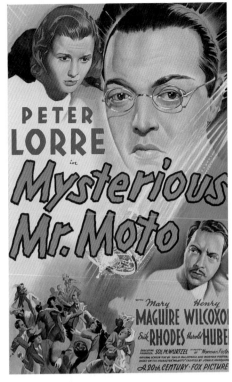

131 **Think Fast, Mr. Moto**, 20th Century Fox, 1937, one-sheet, Cond. B, 41 x 27 in
$600-800

132 **Mr. Moto's Gamble**, 20th Century Fox, 1938, one-sheet, Cond. A-, 41 x 27 in
$600-800

133 **Mysterious Mr. Moto**, 20th Century Fox, 1938, one-sheet, Cond. B+, linenbacked, 41 x 27 in
$500-700

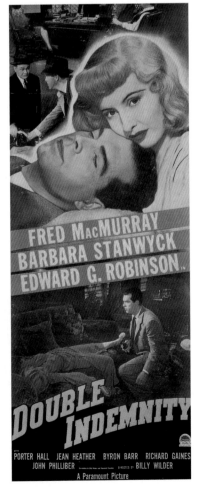

134 **The Postman Always Rings Twice**, MGM, 1946, one-sheet, Cond. A-, 41 x 27 in
$1,500-2,500

135 **The Postman Always Rings Twice**, MGM, 1946, insert, Cond. A, 36 x 14 in
$900-1,200

136 **Double Indemnity**, Paramount, 1944, insert, Cond. A-, 36 x 14 in
$800-1,000

It was the films of tough guys such as Humphrey Bogart and Edward G. Robinson that led to the film noirs of the 1940s. **The Saint** and **The Falcon** were both initially played by George Sanders.

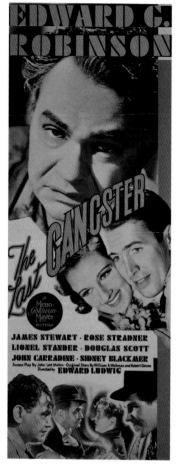

137 **The Last Gangster**, MGM, 1937, insert, Cond. A-, 36 x 14 in $200-400

138 **High Sierra**, Warner Brothers, 1941, insert, Cond. B+, 36 x 14 in $900-1,200

139 **To Have and Have Not**, Warner Brothers, 1944, insert, Cond. A-, 36 x 14 in $600-800

140 **The Saint in London**, RKO, 1939, insert, Cond. B+, 36 x 14 in $200-400

141 **The Gay Falcon**, RKO, 1941, one-sheet, Cond. A-, 41 x 27 in $500-700

142 **A Date with the Falcon**, RKO, 1941, one-sheet, Cond. A, 41 x 27 in $500-700

143 **The Falcon's Brother**, RKO, 1942, one-sheet, Cond. B+, linenbacked, 41 x 27 in $400-600

James Cagney was another famous film tough guy, but he also played a variety of other roles. The studios issued special star portraits of their leading stars, although few survive today.

144 **James Cagney**, Warner Brothers, 1934, special personality poster, Cond. B, 28 x 22 in $700-900

145 **City for Conquest**, Warner Brothers, 1940, insert, Cond. B+, 36 x 14 in $400-600

146 **Strawberry Blonde**, Warner Brothers, 1941, insert, Cond. B+, 36 x 14 in $200-400

147 **Girl Crazy**, MGM, 1943, one-sheet, Cond. B, 41 x 27 in $500-700

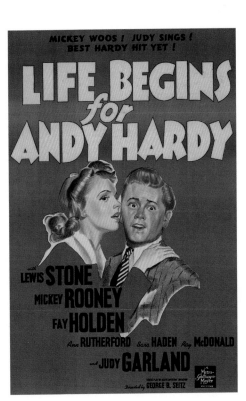

148 **Life Begins for Andy Hardy**, MGM, 1941, one-sheet, Cond. B, 41 x 27 in $400-600

149 **Meet Me in St. Louis**, MGM, 1944, insert, Cond. A-, 36 x 14 in $100-200

After talking films began in 1927, it was only natural that musicals would soon become a leading genre. Astaire & Rogers and MacDonald & Eddy were the most popular musical teams.

150 King of Jazz, Universal, 1930, one-sheet, Cond. A-, 41 x 27 in $900-1,200

151 Follow the Fleet, RKO, 1936, insert, Cond. B, paperbacked, 36 x 14 in $900-1,200

152 Hollywood Party. MGM, 1934, one-sheet, Cond. A, 41 x 27 in $500-700

153 Jeanette MacDonald & Nelson Eddy, MGM, c.1935, 2 special personality posters, Cond. B+, each 28 x 22 in $500-700

Al Jolson, the first talking star, made several memorable films in the 1930s. Many of the leading black stars of the 1930s and 1940s had difficulty getting roles in mainstream films.

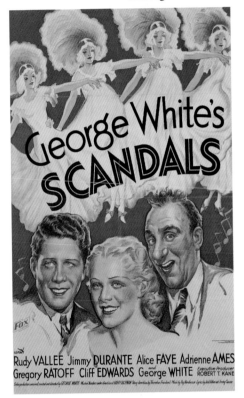

154 **George White's Scandals,** Fox, 1934, one-sheet, Cond. A-, 41 x 27 in $500-700

155 **Swanee River**, 20th Century Fox, 1939, one-sheet, Cond. B+, linenbacked, 41 x 27 in $500-700

156 **Rose of Washington Square**, 20th Century Fox, 1939, one-sheet, Cond. B, linenbacked, 41 x 27 in $500-700

158 **Beware**, Astor, 1946, half-sheet, Cond. B+, 22 x 28 in $100-200

157 **The Big Benefit,** Universal, 1933, one-sheet, Cond. B, 41 x 27 in $400-600

159 **Love Me Tender**, 20th Century Fox, 1956, half-sheet, Cond. B+, 22 x 28 in $150-300

Bob Hope and Bing Crosby made several films in the 1930s before they teamed in the "**Road**" films. Two of the silent cinema's greatest comedy stars were Harold Lloyd and Harry Langdon.

160 Thanks for the Memory, Paramount, 1938, "other company" one-sheet, Cond. B, 41 x 27 in
$400-600

161 Please, Paramount, 1933, one-sheet, Cond. B, 41 x 27 in
$400-600

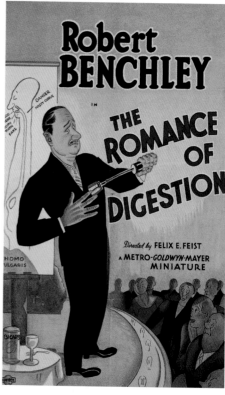

162 The Romance of Digestion, MGM, 1937, one-sheet, Cond. A, 41 x 27 in
$500-700

163 Grandma's Boy, Associated, 1922, one-sheet, Cond. B+, paperbacked, 41 x 27 in
$1,500-2,500

164 Picking Peaches, Pathe, 1924, one-sheet, Cond. B+, linenbacked, 41 x 27 in
$800-1,000

Jail Birds of Paradise is one of two lost Three Stooges films, and includes performances by Moe and an unbilled Curly. The photo offered here was personally signed by Moe, Larry, and Curly.

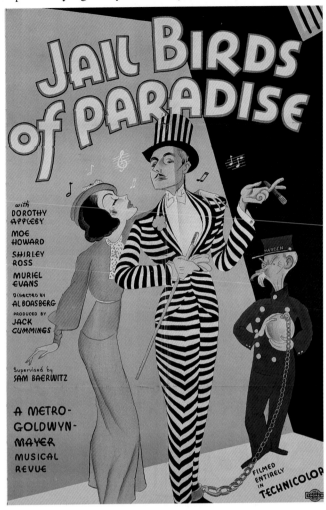

165 **No Father to Guide Him**, Pathe, 1925, one-sheet, Cond. B+, linenbacked, 41 x 27 in $700-900

166 **Jail Birds of Paradise**, MGM, 1934, one-sheet, Cond. A-, 41 x 27 in $1,000-1,500

167 **I'll Be Suing You**, MGM, 1934, one-sheet, Cond. A, 41 x 27 in

$500-700

168 **Three Stooges autographed photo**, 8" x 10" photo, signed by all Three Stooges, framed, Cond. B-,
8 x 10 in $1,000-1,500

The most popular comedy teams of the 1930s were Laurel and Hardy and The Marx Brothers. While Cary Grant is not generally thought of as a comic actor, he had several memorable comic roles.

170 **Bringing Up Baby**, RKO, 1938, insert, Cond. B+, 36 x 14 in $500-700

171 **Arsenic and Old Lace**, Warner Brothers, 1944, insert, Cond. A-, 36 x 14 in $100-200

169 **Laurel and Hardy**, MGM, c.1932, special personality poster, Cond. A-, 28 x 22 in $1,000-1,500

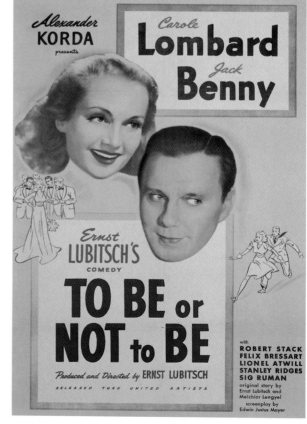

172 **The Big Store**, MGM, 1941, half-sheet, Cond. B+, 22 x 28 in $300-500

173 **To Be or Not To Be**, United Artists, 1942, one-sheet, Cond. A-, 41 x 27 in $400-600

Posters from the prime period of Hal Roach's **Our Gang** comedies, those featuring Spanky and Alfalfa, have always been impossible to find. A remarkable group of five such posters is offered here.

174 **The First Round-Up**, MGM, 1934, one-sheet, Cond. A-, 41 x 27 in　　$1,500-2,500

175 **Three Men in a Tub**, MGM, 1938, one-sheet, Cond. A, 41 x 27 in　　$1,500-2,000

176 **Three Smart Boys**, MGM, 1937, one-sheet, Cond. A, 41 x 27 in　　$1,500-2,000

177 **Pay As You Exit,** MGM, 1936, one-sheet, Cond. A-, 41 x 27 in　　$1,500-2,000

178 **Two Too Young**, MGM, 1936, one-sheet, Cond. A, 41 x 27 in　　$1,500-2,000

France's rich history has inspired countless films. One of the most memorable is **Napoleon**, by Abel Gance. It received a very brief U.S. release, and poster material is virtually unknown.

179 **Napoleon**, MGM, 1926, title lobby card, Cond. A-, 11 x 14 in $2,000-3,000

180 **Scaramouche**, Metro, 1923, six-sheet, Cond. B, linenbacked, 81 x 81 in $1,500-2,500

Ernst Lubitsch was a great European director who came to the United States and created several very memorable films. For a time he was also chief of production at Warner Brothers Studios.

181 **The Rose of Paris**, Universal, 1924, one-sheet, Cond. B+, linenbacked, artwork by Hal Phyfe, 41 x 27 in $500-700

182 **Alias French Gertie**, RKO, 1930, one-sheet, Cond. B+, linenbacked, 41 x 27 in $500-700

183 **So This is Paris**, Warner Brothers, 1926, six-sheet, Cond. B, linenbacked, 81 x 81 in $1,500-2,500

The early 1930s was a time when posters were often works of art, but sadly they are among the rarest of all film posters. Many never before seen titles have surfaced, and are offered here.

184 **Show Boat**, Universal, 1929, one-sheet, Cond. B+, has 2 snipes, 41 x 27 in $1,500-2,500

185 **Abraham Lincoln,** United Artists, 1930, one-sheet, Cond. A-, 41 x 27 in $1,500-2,500

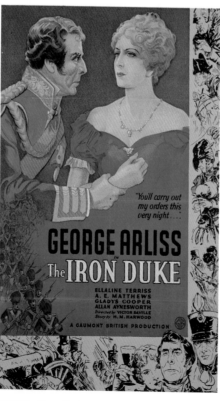

186 **Alexander Hamilton**, Warner Brothers, 1931, one-sheet, Cond. A, 41 x 27 in $1,000-1,500

187 **The Iron Duke**, Gaumont-British, 1934, one-sheet, Cond. A, 41 x 27 in $600-800

188 **Son of India**, MGM, 1931, one-sheet, Cond. B-, linenbacked, 41 x 27 in $600-800

The posters offered on this and the facing page are so rare that until these copies appeared it was not known if even a single copy of many of these posters still survived.

189 **Air Mail**, Universal, 1932, one-sheet, Cond. A-, 41 x 27 in
$600-800

190 **Bird of Paradise**, RKO, 1932, one-sheet, Cond. A-, 41 x 27 in
$1,000-1,500

191 **Chu Chin Chow**, Gaumont-British, 1934, one-sheet, Cond. A-, but right border slightly trimmed, 41 x 27 in
$1,000-1,500

192 **Christina**, Fox, 1929, one-sheet, Cond. B+, 41 x 27 in
$600-800

193 **The Viking**, MGM, 1928, one-sheet, Cond. A-, 41 x 27 in
$600-800

Will Rogers was one of the foremost stars of the cinema from the late-1910s all the way through to his untimely death in 1935. He had his greatest successes after the transition to sound.

194 **A Connecticut Yankee**, Fox, 1931, one-sheet, Cond. B+, linenbacked, 41 x 27 in
$900-1,200

195 **State Fair**, Fox, 1933, one-sheet, Cond. B+, 41 x 27 in
$800-1,000

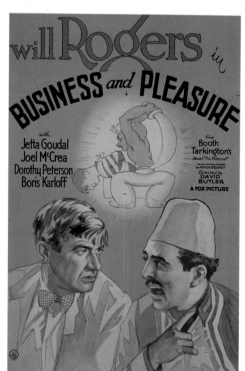

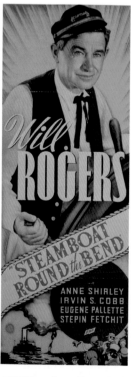

196 **Business and Pleasure**, Fox, 1931, one-sheet, Cond. A-, 41 x 27 in
$600-800

197 **Steamboat Round the Bend**, 20th Century Fox, 1935, insert, Cond. B+, 36 x 14 in
$200-400

198 **The Man Who Broke the Bank at Monte Carlo**, 20th Century Fox, 1935, insert, Cond. B+, 36 x 14 in
$150-300

199 **Treasure Island**, MGM, 1934, insert, Cond. B-, 36 x 14 in
$100-200

200 **Dracula,** Universal, 1931, one-sheet, Cond. A-, 41 x 27 in $60,000-80,000

The posters most valued by collectors have always been those of the 1930s horror films issued by
Universal Studios. The one-sheet of **Dracula** offered here has not had any restoration of any kind.

200 **Dracula,** Universal, 1931, one-sheet, Cond. A-, 41 x 27 in $60,000-80,000

Dracula was Universal's first great sound horror film and original poster material is very rare and desired by collectors. The film spawned several sequels, with some starring the Count's progeny.

201 **Dracula,** Universal, 1931, lobby card, Cond. B, 11 x 14 in $4,000-6,000

202 **Dracula,** Universal, 1931, lobby card, Cond. B+, 11 x 14 in $2,000-3,000

204 **Dracula's Daughter**, Universal, 1936, lobby card, Cond. B+, 11 x 14 in $900-1,200

203 **Dracula,** Universal, 1931, pressbook, plus ad supplement, Cond. B, 21 x 14 in, $3,000-5,000

205 **Son of Dracula**, Universal, 1943, half-sheet, Cond. B, paperbacked, 22 x 28 in $1,000-1,500

Another early Universal success was **The Invisible Man**, from H.G. Wells' novel, and introducing Claude Rains. The one-sheet offered here has not had any restoration of any kind.

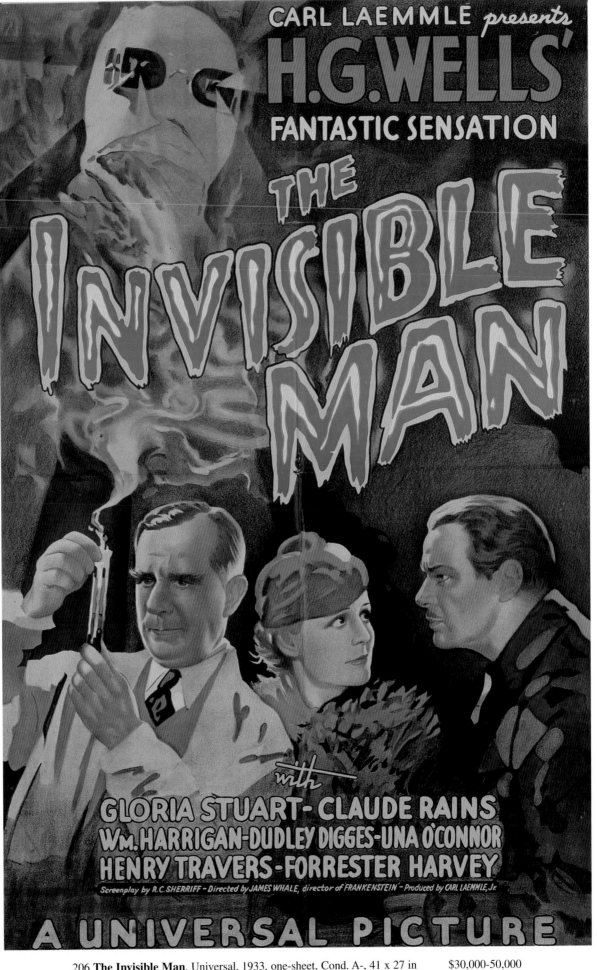

206 **The Invisible Man**, Universal, 1933, one-sheet, Cond. A-, 41 x 27 in $30,000-50,000

It is virtually impossible to get any original poster material from any of the early 1930s Universal horror films, including **Murders in the Rue Morgue**. The two best lobby cards are offered here.

207 **Murders in the Rue Morgue**, Universal, 1932, lobby card, Cond. A-, 11 x 14 in $2,000-3,000

208 **Murders in the Rue Morgue**, Universal, 1932, lobby card, Cond. A-, 11 x 14 in $1,500-2,500

The Raven is a hugely entertaining, yet disturbing film featuring both Karloff and Lugosi. Although lobby cards are virtually never offered for sale, the five best cards are offered here.

209 **The Raven**, Universal, 1935, title lobby card, Cond. B+, 11 x 14 in $5,000-7,000

210 **The Raven**, Universal, 1935, lobby card, Cond. B-,
11 x 14 in $3,000-5,000

212 **The Raven**, Universal, 1935, lobby card, Cond. B,
11 x 14 in $1,000-1,500

211 **The Raven**, Universal, 1935, lobby card, Cond. A-,
11 x 14 in $2,500-3,500

213 **The Raven**, Universal, 1935, lobby card, Cond. A-,
11 x 14 in $1,000-1,500

214 **The Black Cat**, Universal, 1934, title lobby card, Cond. A-, 11 x 14 in $5,000-7,000

The Black Cat is another extremely rare Karloff/Lugosi pairing, and the title card and two scene cards are offered here. Karloff had become typecast in horror roles and performed in little else.

215 **The Black Cat**, Universal, 1934, lobby card,
Cond. A-, 11 x 14 in $2,000-3,000

217 **Juggernaut**, Grand National, 1937, set of 8 lobby cards (1 pictured), Cond. A, 11 x 14 in $700-900

216 **The Black Cat**, Universal, 1934, lobby card,
Cond. B+, 11 x 14 in $1,500-2,500

218 **The Black Room**, AFE Corporation, reissue (date unknown), set of 8 lobby cards (1 pictured), Cond. A, 11 x 14 in $300-500

The Mask of Fu Manchu was a Karloff film made not by Universal. but by MGM. Look closely in these cards and you'll see a very young Myrna Loy, and also Milburn Stone, later Judge Hardy.

219 **The Mask of Fu Manchu**, MGM, 1932, title lobby card, Cond. A-, 11 x 14 in $3,000-4,000

220 **The Mask of Fu Manchu**, MGM, 1932, lobby card, Cond. A-, 11 x 14 in $1,500-2,500

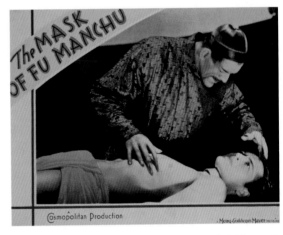

222 **The Mask of Fu Manchu**, MGM, 1932, lobby card, Cond. A-, 11 x 14 in $800-1,000

221 **The Mask of Fu Manchu**, MGM, 1932, lobby card, Cond. B, 11 x 14 in $1,000-1,500

223 **The Mask of Fu Manchu**, MGM, 1932, lobby card, Cond. A-, 11 x 14 in $800-1,000

Conrad Veidt starred in the unsettling film **The Man Who Laughs**. Lon Chaney was the greatest silent star of the silent screen and was set to star in **Dracula** before his untimely death in 1930.

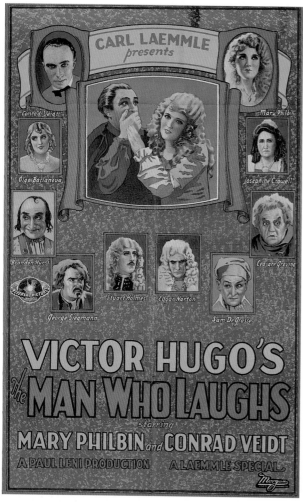

224 The Man Who Laughs, Universal, 1928, one-sheet, Cond. A-, 41 x 27 in $2,000-3,000

225 Lon Chaney, MGM, c.1925, special personality poster, Cond. B, linenbacked, 22 x 28 in $900-1,200

226 The Return of Chandu, Principal, 1934, one-sheet, Cond. B, linenbacked, 41 x 27 in $900-1,200

227 The Devil Bat, PRC, 1940, one-sheet, Cond. A, 41 x 27 in $900-1,200

228 Phantom of the Opera, Universal, 1943, insert, Cond. A, 36 x 14 in $150-300

Greta Garbo was the greatest female star of the 1920s and she handled the transition to sound with ease, remaining immensely popular. Her likeness was all that was needed to sell her films.

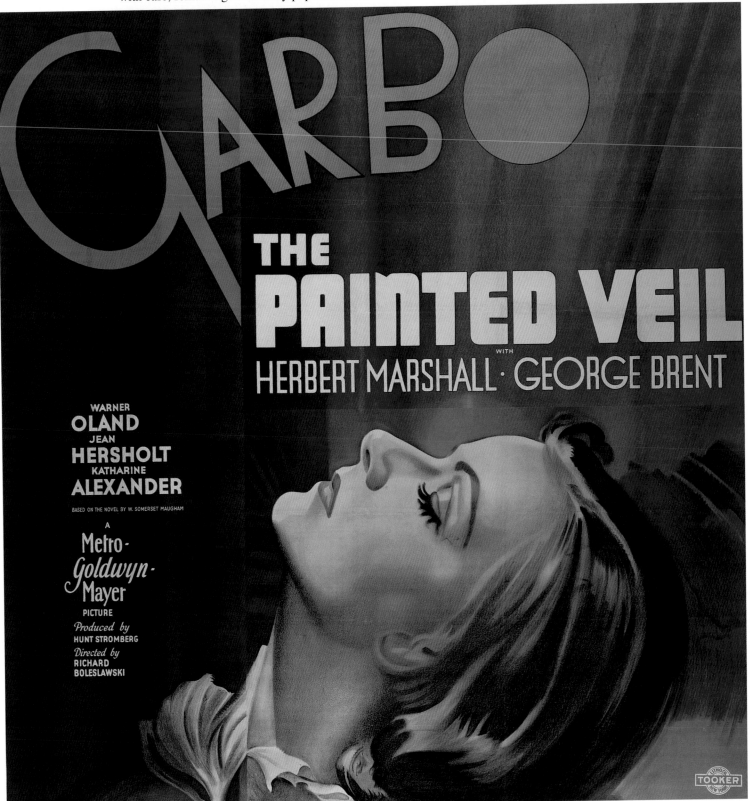

229 **The Painted Veil**, MGM, 1934, six-sheet, Cond. A-, linenbacked, 81 x 81 in $7,000-10,000

Poster artists have always used an attractive likeness of the female star to help lure patrons to the theaters. Often the artists would use their talents to subtly enhance the beauty of these stars.

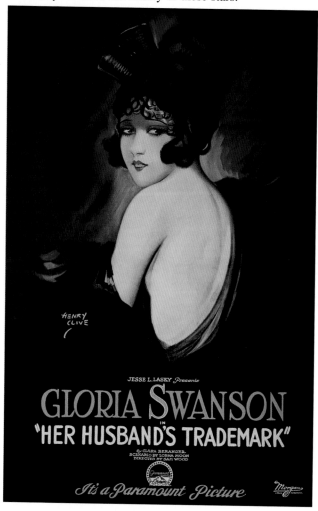

230 **A Woman of Affairs**, MGM, 1928, one-sheet, Cond. A-, linenbacked, 41 x 27 in $4,000-6,000

231 **Her Husband's Trademark,** Paramount, 1922, one-sheet, Cond. B-, linenbacked, 41 x 27 in $3,000-5,000

232 **Smartest Girl in Town**, RKO, 1936, one-sheet, Cond. A-, linenbacked, 41 x 27 in $600-800

233 **Woman of the Year**, MGM, 1942, insert, Cond. A, 36 x 14 in $100-200

234 **Duel in the Sun**, United Artists, 1946, insert, Cond. B+, 36 x 14 in $100-200

The studios issued special star portraits of their leading stars, although few survive today.
The most desired of these are those that depict the greatest female stars of the early 1930s.

235 **Joan Crawford**, MGM, c.1936, special
personality poster, Cond. A-, 28 x 22 in
$900-1,200

236 **Jean Harlow**, MGM, c.1933, special
personality poster, Cond. B, 28 x 22 in
$900-1,200

237 **Marlene Dietrich**, Paramount, 1936,
special personality poster, Cond. B, 28 x 22 in
$900-1,500

238 **She Done Him Wrong**, Paramount, 1933, one-sheet, Cond. B,
linenbacked, 41 x 27 in $3,000-5,000

239 **Love Before Breakfast**, Universal, 1936, one-sheet, Cond. A-,
paperbacked, 41 x 27 in $3,000-5,000

Walt Disney's films were always promoted by the releasing studios, with the single exception of 1937, when the studio issued its own full-color campaign manual, promoting its next year's releases.

240 **1937/38 Disney yearbook,** Walt Disney, 1937/38, yearbook, Cond. A-, 12 x 9 in $500-800

241 **3 Warner Brothers yearbooks,** Warner Brothers 1925/26 (B-), 1926/27 (B), First National 1926/27 (B+) $500-800

242 **4 Paramount yearbooks,** 1929/30 (B), 1932/33 (B+), 1934/35 (B-), 1937/38 (B) $800-1,200

Each year studios would release elaborate campaign books designed to sell theater owners on their upcoming films. Often they promoted films whose titles, plots, or stars later changed.

243 **Universal 1931/32 yearbook**, Cond. B, 14.5 x 10.5 in $800-1,200

244 **6 RKO yearbooks,** 1933/34 (C, pages out), 1939/40 (B), 1940/41 (B+), 1941/42 (B+), 1942/43 (B), 1943/44 (B) $1,200-1,800

In 1942, MGM, the most successful studio, began publishing a bi-monthly (later monthly) magazine, **Lion's Roar**, packed with information and art. A near-complete collection of these rare magazines is offered.

245 **2 MGM yearbooks,** 1926/27 (B), 1927/28 (B+) $400-700

246 **10 Lion's Roar magazines**, MGM, the first ten issues, 1941 to June 1942, Cond. A- to C (one coverless) $1,000-2,000

247 **9 Lion's Roar magazines,** MGM, nine issues from #11 (7/42) to Vol. III #4 (7/44), Cond A to B- $1,000-2,000

248 **10 Lion's Roar magazines**, MGM, ten issues from Vol. III #5 (12/44) to Vol. V #4 (8/46), Cond. A- to B- $1,000-1,500

249 **4 Fox yearbooks,** 1923/24 (A), 1925/26 (A), 1926/27 (B), April 1945 (B) $800-1,200

William Holden started a scrapbook while appearing in a community theater in 1938. He was signed to a Hollywood contract, and starred in **Golden Boy**. His personal scrapbook, complete with his first three contracts (he was paid $50 a week!), his first fan letter, and much much more is offered here. This is a remarkable artifact from one of the finest American film actors.

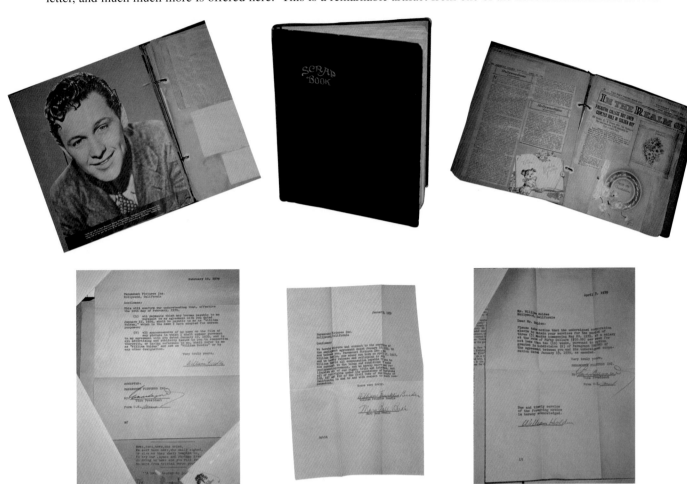

250 **William Holden's scrapbook**, 1938/1939, personally compiled by William Holden, Cond. B+ $2,000-4,000

251 **4 Columbia yearbooks**, 1932/33 (B-), 1934/35 (B), 1940/41 (B), 1940/41, Serials, Shorts, and Westerns (B+)
$800-1,200

Before Shirley Temple became a leading star at the age of six, she appeared in a series of short films. Two exceedingly rare one-sheets are offered, as well as a set of four lobby cards.

252 **Boom Town**, MGM, 1940, one-sheet, Cond. B, linenbacked, 41 x 27 in
$1,000-1,500

253 **Lloyds of London**, 20th Century Fox, 1936, one-sheet, Cond. B+, paperbacked, 41 x 27 in
$2,000-3,000

254 **Pardon My Pups**, Fox, 1933, one-sheet and set of 4 lobby cards (2 pictured), Cond. A to B-, 41 x 27 in and 11 x 14 in
$1,000-1,500

255 **Managed Money**, Fox, 1934, one-sheet, Cond. A, 41 x 27 in
$600-800

Most of the posters that exist from before 1915 are the only example of that poster. Many of these are historically and artistically memorable, yet most are still surprisingly affordable.

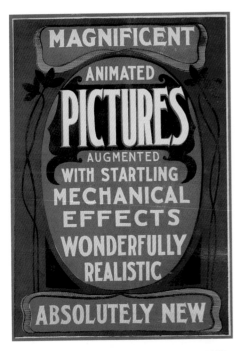

256 **Magnificent Animated Pictures**, c.1900, half-sheet, Cond. B, linenbacked, 41 x 27 in
$400-600

257 **High Class Moving Pictures**, Lyman Howes, c.1909, half-sheet, Cond. A-, paperbacked, 41 x 27 in
$200-300

258 **His Ancestors**, Edison, 1913, one-sheet, Cond. B+, linenbacked, 41 x 27 in
$500-700

259 **The Younger Brothers**, Longhorn Co., c.1905, three-sheet, Cond. C, linenbacked, 81 x 41 in
$900-1,200

260 **Neptune's Daughter**, Universal, 1914, three-sheet, Cond. B-, linenbacked, 81 x 41 in
$1,000-1,500

261 **The Bottle Imp**, Paramount, 1917, three-sheet, Cond. B+, linenbacked, 81 x 41 in
$900-1,200

The Perils of Pauline is the best-remembered serial of all time. **A Lady of Quality** and **Burning Daylight** were made by the studios that soon evolved into Paramount Pictures.

262 **The Passion Play of Ober-Ammergau**, c.1898, one-sheet, Cond. B+, linenbacked, 41 x 27 in $1,000-1,500

263 **The Perils of Pauline**, Eclectic, 1914, one-sheet, Cond. A-, linenbacked, 41 x 27 in $5,000-7,000

264 **A Lady of Quality**, Paramount, 1914, one-sheet, Cond. B, linenbacked, 41 x 27 in $900-1,200

265 **Burning Daylight**, Paramount, 1914, one-sheet, Cond. B+, linenbacked, 41 x 27 in $900-1,200

266 **Today in Samoa**, Paramount, c.1920, one-sheet, Cond. B+, linenbacked, 41 x 27 in $500-700

D.W. Griffith's **The Birth of a Nation** was one of the only silent films to be selected to the AFI's list of the 100 Greatest American films. The one-sheet offered is one of two known copies.

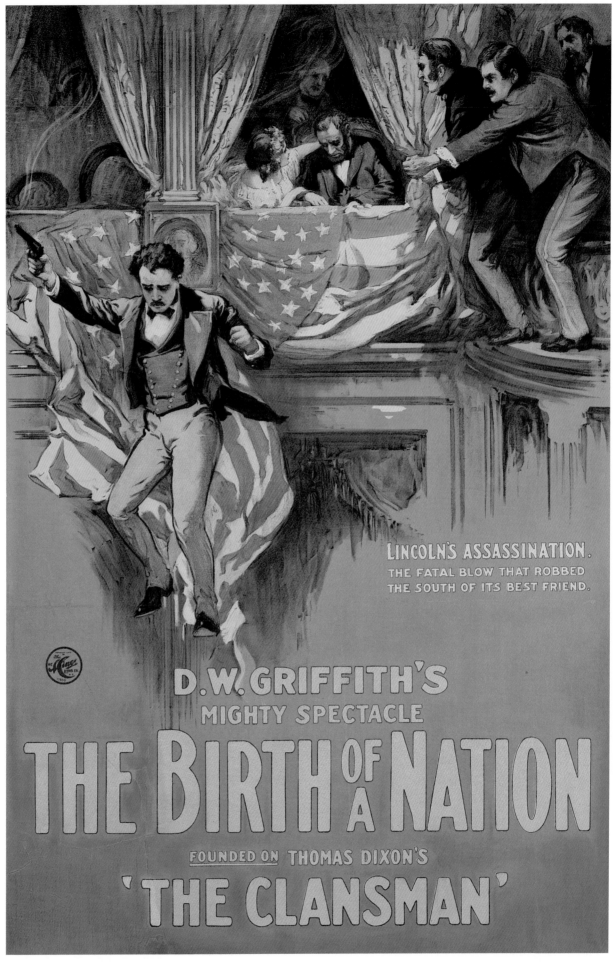

267 **The Birth of a Nation**, Epoch, 1915, one-sheet, Cond. B-, linenbacked, 41 x 27 in $15,000-20,000

Cecil B. DeMille and Erich Von Stroheim were two of the greatest directors of silent films.
Posters from any of their silent films are extremely rare, expecially three-sheets and six-sheets.

268 **Manslaughter**, Paramount, 1922, six-sheet, Cond. B-, linenbacked, 81 x 81 in $1,000-1,500

269 **The Merry Widow**, MGM, 1925, three-sheet, Cond. B-, linenbacked, 81 x 41 in $2,000-3,000

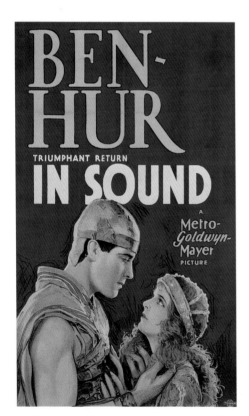

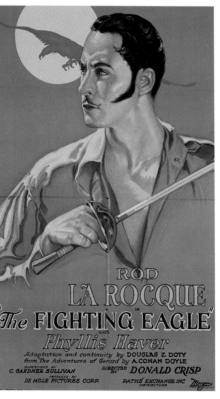

270 **Ben-Hur,** MGM, R1930, one-sheet, Cond. B+, linenbacked, 41 x 27 in $700-900

271 **The Fighting Eagle**, Pathe, 1927, one-sheet, Cond. A, 41 x 27 in $600-800

272 **Uncle Tom's Cabin**, Universal, 1927, one-sheet, Cond. B+, 41 x 27 in $800-1,000

The silent version of **The Thief of Bagdad** was Douglas Fairbanks' greatest film, and several different one-sheets were created. Perhaps the finest of these, depicting the flying carpet, is offered.

273 **The Thief of Bagdad**, United Artists, 1924, one-sheet, Cond. B+, linenbacked, 41 x 27 in
$15,000-20,000

Original material from 1930s United Artists' films, such as **Hell's Angels**, is extremely rare because the studio only handled the inital release of its films and then let other companies distribute them.

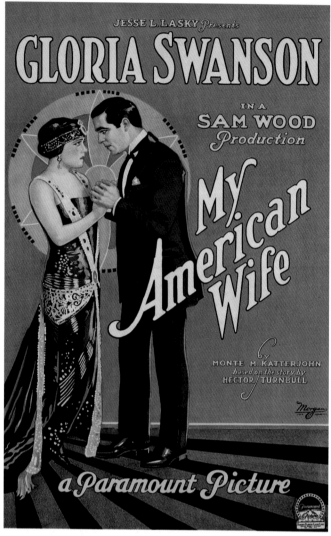

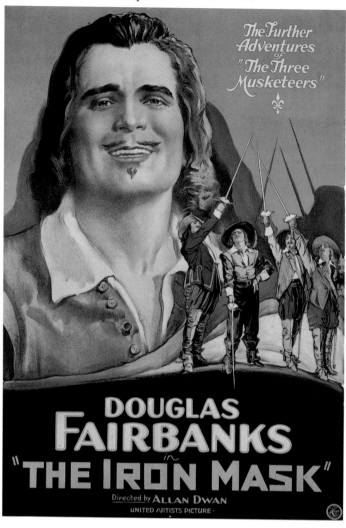

274 **My American Wife**, Paramount, 1922, one-sheet, Cond. A-, linenbacked, 41 x 27 in $2,000-3,000

275 **The Iron Mask**, United Artists, 1929, one-sheet, Cond. B, linenbacked, 41 x 27 in $2,000-3,000

276 **Hell's Angels**, United Artists, 1930, half-sheet, Cond. C, paperbacked, 22 x 28 in $1,000-1,500

277 **All Quiet on the Western Front**, Universal, 1934 reissue, one-sheet, Cond. A, 41 x 27 in $600-800

Gone With the Wind was such a success that it was immediately re-issued, and consequently original posters are very rare. The "kiss" style one-sheet offered is in immaculate condition.

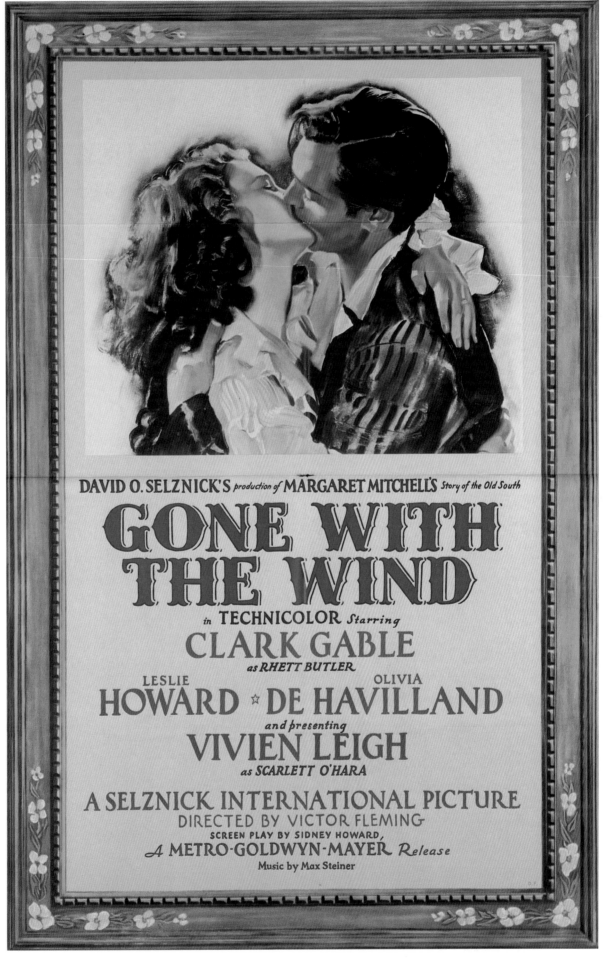

278 **Gone With the Wind**, MGM, 1939, one-sheet, Cond. A, 41 x 27 in $8,000-10,000

Never before has so much original **Gone With the Wind** poster material been
offered at one time. None of the pieces have had the slighest restoration.

279 **Gone With the Wind**, MGM, 1939, one-sheet,
Cond. B+, 41 x 27 in $6,000-8,000

280 **Gone With the Wind**, MGM, 1939, one-sheet,
Cond. A-, 41 x 27 in $2,500-3500

281 **Gone With the Wind**,
MGM, 1939, insert, Cond. B,
36 x 14 in $4,000-6,000

282 **Gone With the Wind**, MGM, 1939,
7 lobby cards (2 pictured), Cond. B+ to B-,
each 11 x 14 in $1,000-1,500

283 **The Magnificent Ambersons**,
RKO, 1942, insert, Cond. B,
36 x 14 in $300-500

Recently, the American Film Institute chose the 100 greatest American films ever made, and **Citizen Kane** was chosen first, as it has been in virtually every poll since the film was first released. The six-sheet offered, one of two known copies, perfectly captures the theme of the film, the search for the key to unlock the seemingly contradictory sides of Charles Foster Kane.

284 **Citizen Kane**, RKO, 1941, six-sheet, Cond. A-, linenbacked, 81 x 81 in $15,000-20,000

John Barrymore was an astonishingly gifted actor, and he was equally capable of playing
a suave jewel thief in **Arsene Lupin**, or an absent-minded professor in **Topaze**.

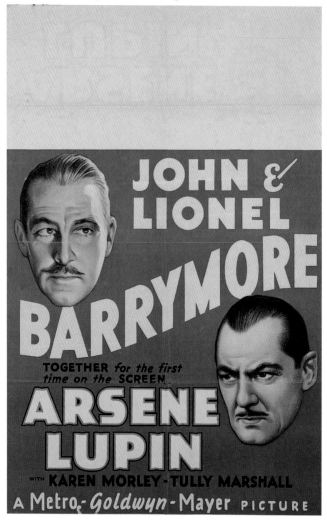

285 **Topaze**, RKO, 1933, one-sheet, Cond. A-, 41 x 27 in
$1,500-2,500

286 **Arsene Lupin**, MGM, 1932, one-sheet, Cond. A-, 41 x 27 in
$800-1,000

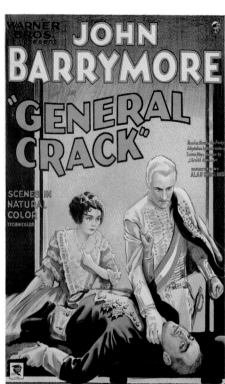

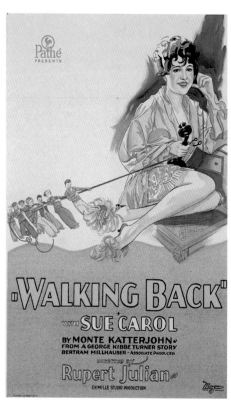

287 **General Crack**, Warner Brothers, 1930,
one-sheet, Cond. B+, linenbacked, 41 x 27 in
$900-1,200

288 **Noah's Ark**, Warner Brothers, 1929,
one-sheet, Cond. B+, 41 x 27 in $600-800

289 **Walking Back**, Pathe, 1928, one-sheet,
Cond. A-, 41 x 27 in $600-800

There have been hundreds of Tarzan films, but none as memorable as **Tarzan the Ape Man**.
Until the one-sheet offered here surfaced, it was thought that not a single copy survived.

290 **Tarzan the Ape Man**, MGM, 1932, one-sheet, Cond. A-, 41 x 27 in $8,000-12,000

The Tarzan the Mighty poster offered here is the only known copy. It had each of the four corners trimmed, but they have been expertly restored.

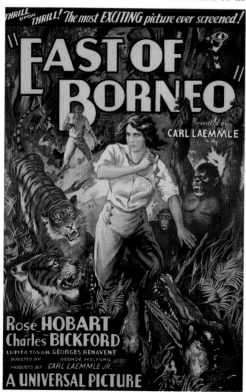

291 **East of Borneo**, Universal, 1931, one-sheet, Cond. A, linenbacked, 41 x 27 in $1,000-1,500

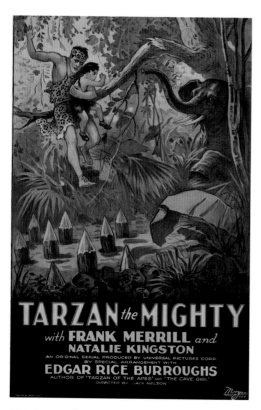

292 **Tarzan the Mighty**, Universal, 1928, one-sheet, Cond. C+, linenbacked, 41 x 27 in $4,000-6,000

293 **Attack of the 50 ft. Woman**, Allied Artists, 1958, three-sheet, Cond. A, linenbacked, 81 x 41 in $1,500-2,500

One-sheets from the serial films of **Superman** and **Batman** have always been very desirable.
Also popular are the posters from the 1950s sci-fi films, such as **Attack of the 50 ft. Woman**.

294 **Superman**, Columbia, 1948, one-sheet, Cond. B+, 41 x 27 in
$1,000-1,500

295 **New Adventures of Batman & Robin**, Columbia, 1949,
one-sheet, Cond. B+, 41 x 27 in
$900-1,200

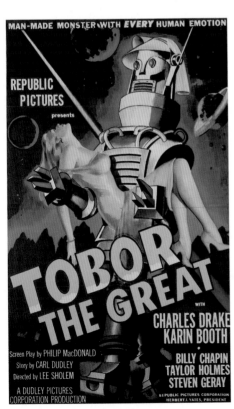

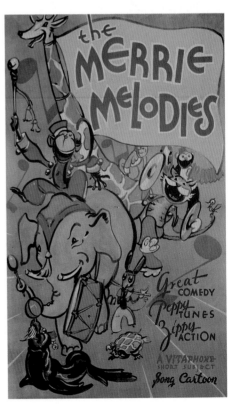

296 **Tobor the Great,** Republic, 1954,
one-sheet, Cond. A-, 41 x 27 in
$500-700

297 **King of the Rocket Men**, Republic, 1949,
one-sheet, Cond. B+, 41 x 27 in
$600-800

298 **The Merrie Melodies**, Vitaphone, c.1932,
one-sheet, Cond. A-, 41 x 27 in
$800-1,200

An immaculate copy of the **Pinocchio** one-sheet is offered here. **Morning, Noon and Night** is one of the only surviving pre-code Betty Boop posters, complete with her garter and suggestive title.

299 **Pinocchio**, RKO, 1940, one-sheet, Cond. A, 41 x 27 in
$4,000-6,000

300 **Morning, Noon and Night,** Paramount, 1933, one-sheet,
Cond. B+, paperbacked, 41 x 27 in $4,000-6,000

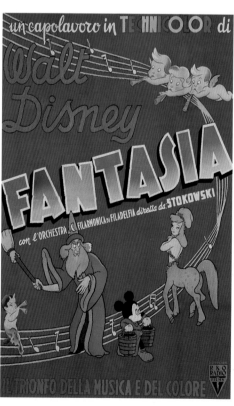

301 **Bambi**, RKO, c. 1950, Italian poster,
Cond. A, linenbacked, 55 x 78 in $800-1,200

302 **Fantasia**, RKO, 1952, Italian poster,
Cond. A, linenbacked, 55 x 78 in $800-1,200

303 **Me Musical Nephews**, Paramount, 1941,
one-sheet, Cond. B+, linenbacked, 41 x 27 in
$500-700

While some studios issued stock posters for many of their cartoons, Columbia made an attractive poster for each of its Color Rhapsodies. **Willie Whopper** was created by the great Ub Iwerks.

304 **Snowtime**, Columbia, 1938, one-sheet, Cond. A, 41 x 27 in $500-700

305 **Bluebirds' Baby**, Columbia, 1938, one-sheet, Cond. A, 41 x 27 in $400-600

306 **Hollywood Picnic**, Columbia, 1937, one-sheet, Cond. A, 41 x 27 in $400-600

307 **Willie Whopper**, MGM, 1933, one-sheet, Cond. A-, 41 x 27 in $1,500-2,500

308 **Uncle Tom's Cabana**, MGM, 1947, one-sheet, Cond. A-, paperbacked, 41 x 27 in $700-900

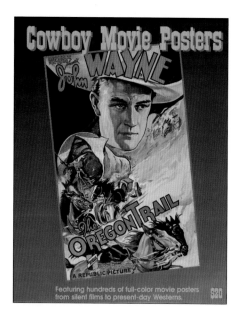

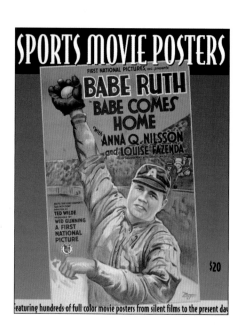

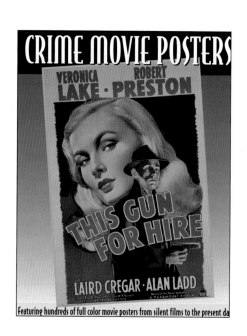

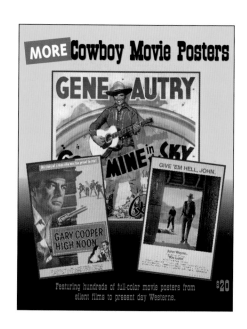

If you enjoy this catalog you're holding in your hands, you're sure to enjoy the other 16 full-color books of movie posters that Bruce Hershenson has published. Pictured on this page are the covers of the seven volumes of Bruce's series, The Illustrated History of Movies Through Posters. All are at least 84 pages of full-color, and each contain at least 300 reproductions of great film posters from a single genre, arranged chronologically from early silents through the present day. Each is still available for the original cover price of $20 each, and can be ordered through your local bookstore (if they don't have them in stock, they can special order them for you). Or you can order direct from the publisher at the address, phone, fax, or web site below.

Mail: Bruce Hershenson, P.O. Box 874, West Plains, MO 65775
Phone: (417) 256 9616 • Fax: (417) 257 6948
Web Site: http://www.brucehershenson.com

This auction was organized by Howard Lowery and Bruce Hershenson.

Howard Lowery is the owner of the Howard Lowery Gallery in Burbank, California, and in the last ten years Howard has held over thirty auctions that have cumulatively sold over twenty million dollars of animation art, comic books, comic art, movie memorabilia and posters, and all sorts of other collectibles. If you have collectibles you would like to consign to a future Howard Lowery auction, you should contact him at the address or phone number found on the first page of this catalog. If you are interested in purchasing collectibles, contact Howard to find out about his upcoming auctions.

Bruce Hershenson is the world's foremost vintage movie poster dealer. Since 1989 he has been a full-time movie poster   dealer, and from 1990 to 1997 he was Christie's auction house's movie poster expert, organizing ten movie poster auctions that had cumulative sales of over nine million dollars. He has issued 14 semi-annual sales catalogs with total sales of over three million dollars. He has published 17 full-color books of movie poster reproductions. Together with partner Richard Allen (co-author of Reel Art), Bruce owns the Hershenson-Allen archive, which contains over 25,000 color transparencies of vintage movie posters covering all years and subjects, available for use in books, magazines or videos. In 1998, Bruce opened his website, http://www.brucehershenson.com, and it is the most visited vintage movie poster site on the Internet. It contains hundreds of images of vintage film posters, and is packed with information that every collector needs to know. If you are looking to buy or sell movie posters, you should   contact Bruce in any of the following ways:

Mail: Bruce Hershenson, P.O. Box 874, West Plains, MO 65775
Phone: (417) 256 9616 • Fax: (417) 257 6948
Web Site: http://www.brucehershenson.com

This auction will be held at the Feldman Gallery of the PACIFIC DESIGN CENTER in Beverly Hills, California. Directions to the Pacific Design Center are as follows:

We are located at the intersection of San Vicente Blvd. and Melrose Ave. Enter the parking structure at either Melrose Ave. or San Vicente Blvd. Enter at San Vicente Blvd. only after 5 PM, Monday - Friday.

Directions from the following freeways:

1. **Harbor Freeway (11) - Southeast of PDC** (from either direction).
   Harbor Freeway to Santa Monica Freeway (10) West.
   EXIT at La Cienega Blvd North - Proceed 5 miles.
   LEFT at Melrose Ave. - PDC is 3 miles down on the right.

2. **Hollywood Freeway (101) - East of PDC** (from either direction).
   EXIT at Highland Ave. South - Proceed 2 miles.
   RIGHT at Melrose Ave. - PDC is 3 miles down on the right.

3. **Pasadena Freeway (110) - Northeast of PDC.**
   From Pasadena - Pasadena Freeway (110) to Hollywood Freeway (101) North. EXIT at Melrose Ave. West - Proceed 5 miles PDC is on the right.

4. **San Diego Freeway (405) - West of PDC** (from either direction).
   EXIT at Santa Monica Blvd. East - Proceed 5 miles.
   RIGHT at San Vicente Blvd. - PDC is 2 blocks down on the left.

5. **Santa Monica Freeway (10) - South of PDC** (from either direction)
   EXIT at La Cienega Blvd. North - Proceed 5 miles.
   LEFT at Melrose Ave. - PDC is 3 blocks down on the right.

6. **Santa Ana Freeway (5) - Southeast of PDC.**
   Santa Ana Freeway North to Santa Monica Freeway (10) West.
   EXIT at La Cienega Blvd. North - Proceed 5 miles.
   LEFT at Melrose Ave. - PDC is 3 blocks down on the right.

7. **Ventura Freeway (134) - Northeast of PDC (Glendale) via Laurel Canyon.**
   Ventura Freeway (134) North becomes Ventura Freeway (101).
   EXIT at Laurel Canyon Ave. South - Proceed 5 miles through the canyon.
   At Sunset Blvd. Laurel Canyon becomes Crescent Heights Blvd. - Proceed 1 mile. RIGHT at Melrose Ave. - Proceed 1 mile PDC is on the right.

8. **Ventura Freeway (101) – Northwest of PDC (Encino) via San Diego Freeway**
   East or West of San Diego Freeway - to San Diego Freeway South.
   EXIT at Santa Monica Blvd East - Proceed
   RIGHT at San Vicente Blvd. - PDC is 1 block down on the left.

9. **Ventura Freeway (101) - at North of PDC (Studio City) via Hollywood Freeway**.
   Ventura Freeway South becomes Hollywood Freeway (101) South.
   EXIT at Highland Ave. South - Proceed 2 miles.
   RIGHT at Melrose Ave. - PDC is 3 miles down on the right.

If you have any special needs related to this auction (bidding, previews, and so forth) please contact either Howard Lowery or Bruce Hershenson, and they will do everything possible to accommodate you.

VINTAGE HOLLYWOOD POSTERS INDEX